access to relig

INTRODUCTION TO THE NEW TESTAMENT

Kevin O'Donnell

Hodder & Stoughton

A MEMBER OF THE HODDER HEADLINE GROUP

Some other titles in the series:

Issues of Life and Death
Michael Wilcockson ISBN 0 340 72488 9

Philosophy of Religion
Peter Cole ISBN 0 340 72491 9

Future titles in the series:

Religion and Science
Mel Thompson ISBN 0 340 75771 X

Sex and Relationships
Michael Wilcockson ISBN 0 340 72489 7

Environmental Ethics
Joe Walker ISBN 0 340 75770 1

Acknowledgements

The Publishers and the Author would like to thank the following for permission to reproduce copyright photographs in this book: Figure 1, p. 25 and Figure 2, p. 29, AKG Photos; Figure 4, p. 52, Alex Keene.

Orders: please contact Bookpoint Ltd, 130 Milton Park, Abingdon, Oxon OX14 4SB. Telephone: (44) 01235 827720, Fax: (44) 01235 400454. Lines are open from 9.00–6.00, Monday to Saturday, with a 24 hour message answering service. Email address: orders@bookpoint.co.uk

British Library Cataloguing in Publication Data
A catalogue for this title is available from The British Library

ISBN 0 340 72490 0
First published 1999

Impression number 10 9 8 7 6 5 4 3 2
Year 2005 2004 2003 2002 2001

Cover photo from AKG photos.

Typeset by Transet Ltd, Coventry, England
Printed in Great Britain for Hodder & Stoughton educational, a division of Hodder Headline Plc, 338, Euston Road, London NW1 3BH by The Bath Press, Bath

Contents

Preface

To the general reader

Although *Access* books have been designed mainly to meet the needs of examination students, they also have much to offer the general reader. *Access* authors are committed to writing up-to-date scholarly texts in an easily accessible format. The main body of the text should therefore provide a readable and engaging survey of the subject, in easily digestible sections. Clarity is further enhanced by sub-headings and bulletpoints.

To the student reader

Access books are written mainly for students studying for examinations at higher level, particularly GCE Advanced Subsidiary (AS) Level and Advanced (A) Level. A number of features have been included to assist students, such as the word-lists at the beginning of chapters and the material at the end of chapters.

To use this book most effectively, you should be aware of the following features.

- The introductory chapter will set the scene for the material in the rest of the book.
- The Contents gives a break-down of the sections in each chapter.
- If you turn to the relevant chapters, you will find that they are broken down further into sub-headings and bulletpoints. There are sometimes also Key Issues to focus your attention on important points.
- The Key Words at the beginning of each chapter are for easy reference and to help you become more familiar with the technical language of the subject.
- At the end of each chapter is a summary of the main points, presented either as lists or diagrams. This is a useful quick revision tool. The list can also form the outline of your own notes on the topic.
- There may be some suggestions for further reading on the topic.
- There is also a range of typical examination questions, with some specific advice on how to answer them. Do tackle the specimen questions, planning your answers to some of them and writing some in full.

General advice on answering essay questions
Structured questions will tell you what to include. The following advice is for those questions which leave it to you to work out.

- The most important thing is to read the question carefully and work out what it really means. Make sure you understand all the words in the question (you may need to check some of them in the dictionary or look up technical terms in the Word Lists in the book).

- Gather the relevant information for answering the question. You will probably *not* need everything you know on the topic. Keep to what the question is asking.
- Organise your material by drawing up a plan of paragraphs. Make sure that each paragraph is relevant to the question. Include different views within your answer (most questions require arguments for and against).
- Start with an introduction which explains in your own words what the question is asking and defines any technical words. Work through your answer in your carefully planned paragraphs. Write a brief conclusion in which you sum up your answer to the question (without repeating everything in the essay).

1 The Christ 'Myth'

KEYWORDS

apocalyptic – revealing the future

Christ – Greek form of 'Messiah' in Hebrew, meaning 'anointed one'. The coming king, foretold by Old Testament prophets.

demythologising – reinterpreting supernatural stories in the Gospels as philosophical truths

existentialism – philosophy concerned with human life and its meaning

Exodus – escape of the Hebrew slaves from Egypt

Hellenistic – description of world under Greek influence. Greek was spoken as an international language in the Roman Empire. Not everyone spoke Latin

incarnation – 'in a body' – God made man

ineffable – beyond words and human description

Kingdom of God – God's rule on earth, a time of peace and blessing

Messiah – God's chosen, anointed King and coming deliverer

mystery cults – secret societies that sought immortality through religious rituals

myth – symbolic story containing spiritual truth

rabbi – Jewish religious teacher, specially trained in the Law of Moses

Yahweh – sacred name for God in Judaism, meaning something like 'I am who I am'

1 Introduction

KEY ISSUE The New Testament (NT) was a product of a new religious movement that burst upon the ancient world with vigour and freshness; but it was not a movement born in a religious and cultural vacuum. The first century AD was a period of much soul-searching in which a number of new religious groups became popular in the Roman Empire.

Some of these new religions involved the old Graeco-Roman gods, others were based upon Eastern cults and myths; and the speculations of the philosophers were debated and followed by the learned. Despite the basic social stability enforced by Roman legions, many wondered what the purpose of life really was, and searched for a spiritual salvation. Others were oppressed by the mighty Roman Empire and struggled for a political salvation, for freedom and independence. Both of these currents were at work within Galilee and Judaea in the first century. Though the Old Testament (OT) and the traditions of the Jewish **rabbis** formed the cradle of Christianity, its nursery was the rich and fertile mixture of customs and traditions in the **Hellenistic** world, because of the cultural unity imposed by Rome.

The figure of Jesus of Nazareth, a Galilean Jew and wandering prophet/teacher with his band of disciples, walked across this landscape and was influenced by it. Indeed, studying how much he was a child of his time will also suggest how original and how striking he must have been. The early Christians responded to him, often to the point of enduring torture, exile or martyrdom, by developing a cult of their own which eventually separated from Judaism (although this was probably not the original intention). This cult promised salvation, a coming **Kingdom**, and proclaimed the crucified teacher as the risen Lord and **Messiah**.

The influences at work in the formation of Christianity, and the passionate vision of God meeting humanity in love and forgiveness in Jesus Christ, summing up all their hopes of liberation, is an intricate story that in the following pages we can only begin to unfold. The way modern people make sense of the writings, beliefs and hopes of the early Christians is controversial and must also be reflected upon. Some of the old terminology does not resonate in the way that it once did. To call Jesus the Messiah, for example, was a striking, daring claim for the first Christians to make, but what does it mean for Christians today? The issue of miracles is also one that is keenly debated by modern theologians. Engaging the text of the New Testament should not be only a historical exercise, seeing what an ancient group of people believed; it should also challenge you to explore your own hopes and fears and to view your own beliefs in the light of theirs.

2 Myths

KEY ISSUE The New Testament contains ideas which seem odd or unscientific today. God comes to earth in a man (through a virgin birth), miracles are performed, devils are cast out, the God-man rises from the dead and lives forever. One day, he will come again in power and glory, with all the angels, to remake the world and judge everyone.

We can try to go behind the text and study the people, movements and influences that formed this grand narrative. We can look at Jesus in his context as a historical figure of the first century AD. To be scholarly, we must do so, and yet, we must never lose sight of the fact that the New Testament is an epic tale. It engages universals and deep yearnings and feelings within us. It uses mythology, but this should not be seen as something for the conceptual scrapheap.

Myth can mean many things. The common understanding of it is that it is outmoded, pre-scientific thought. It was the way the ancients explained the world, and myths were about primordial truths – the foundation of the universe in a distant, timeless time, 'in the beginning'. Yet, myth can also be about universal, human truths and mysteries. It is a symbolic story that resonates in every age because it is pointing beyond its form to something in reality, in the nature of things. Life cannot just be summed up by physical forces and chemical equations. Truth, beauty, value, compassion, awe and mystery cannot be tied down so easily. If the universe has become aware of itself in human beings, then myths are expressive of their place within it. Perhaps we need powerful stories to focus our minds on these aspects of a 'moreness' to life than eating, drinking and sleeping. Sometimes, myths can express truth better than logical analysis.

This sense of myth came more into its own in the twentieth century with psychoanalysis and dream symbols. Jung made a connection between ancient myths and dreams, seeing deep seated, universal, archetypal images in them.

> No science will ever replace myth, and a myth cannot be made out of any science. For it is not that 'God' is a myth, but that myth is the revelation of a divine life in man. It is not we who invent myth, rather it speaks to us as a Word of God.
>
> *Memories, Dreams and Reflections*, Fontana, 1963, p. 373

This sentiment is echoed by another scholar, G.S. Kirk:

> The primitive mentality does not invent myths, it experiences them.
>
> *Myth: Its Meaning and Functions in Ancient and Other Cultures*, Cambridge, 1970, p. 279

Humans need good stories and myths to inspire them. Works of art, music, films and novels that utilise mythological themes are still powerful today. Hence Norse mythology shines out in Wagner's *Ring Cycle* and still enthrals. Tolkien's stories for children in *The Lord of the Rings* grip us with their own mythical tales and reworkings of classical themes – the journey, temptation, the personification of evil, raw beauty and holiness. Films such as *Star Wars* use old symbols with hi-tech equipment, as swords turn into light sabres, and good struggles against evil, light against darkness. Do we follow modern myths today?

For example, was Marxism a myth? What about media stars and attitudes to them? How far can technology be seen in mythical terms? One of the inventors of the atomic bomb quoted Hindu mythology when he saw it explode: 'I am become the destroyer of the worlds'.

A moot point, though, is whether all talk about God has to be considered as mythological. We can only speak of the divine in symbolic and analogous terms, as we are dealing with ideas of the Beyond, the **ineffable**, and language becomes stretched. Myth, strictly speaking, should be a story, a dramatic narrative, that uses such symbols. 'God' might be said to be a symbol of the Ground of our Being, Ultimate Reality, the Love at the heart of the universe; but a myth about God will have him moving and doing something.

We can be self-conscious of myth in Christianity and still enjoy its pulling power. C S Lewis argued that it would be surprising if there was no myth in the New Testament, for if **Christ** was epic, universal, and not just local, temporal and historical, then he must be dressed in mythical language. Indeed, Lewis went as far as to say that Christ was the fulfilment of ancient myths: myth become fact as the **incarnation** made a thousand dying and rising nature gods real, historical.

The ancients had worshipped and told stories about many dying and rising gods, such as Balder and Osiris. A radical difference between the Christ myth and the myths of the Classical world is that the latter never actually happened – they were poetic descriptions of universals. 'This never happened, but always is.' Hence life is a continual process of death and rebirth. With Christ, this did happen. The early Christians saw their new myth as based upon bedrock, historical, particular events. Jesus lived in a certain time and place, and not a timeless age. This is the oddness of Christianity. What caused so much to be said of just one man in history?

It is worth reflecting upon the myths that were influential in the **Hellenistic** and Jewish world. The New Testament is influenced by these, though it radically transforms them in various ways.

3 Hellenistic myths

a) The appearance of a god

Myths were full of tales of a god appearing in human form, either to trick a woman into having sex with him, or to give a message to a mortal. They did not really take flesh and blood, it was only an apparition. In the New Testament, God really became man, and suffered on the cross.

b) The demigods

Mythical figures such as Heracles were part god/part human, the offspring of a god and a mortal mother. Jesus was said to be God and Man, but not as a hybrid creature. God lived in him, uniquely.

c) Good men were taken into heaven

Classical mythology reserved heaven for the gods. Mortals lived on in the Underworld, Hades. Now and then, a wise, holy person gained the favour of the gods and was promoted to join the immortals. Jesus was a man raised up to heaven, but a representative man, opening the way for all.

d) The Cosmic Man

Experts speculate on the existence of a Primal or Cosmic Man myth in the ancient world, from which humans were the offspring. This occurs in later writings, but may have been around before Christ. In some later forms of this, the Cosmic Man descended into the world to enlighten people who each carried a piece of the divine light within them. Paul toys with a similar idea in 1 Corinthians 15:45 with his First Adam/Last Adam ideas, whereby Christ is a new model that affects the whole of humanity. Seeing the risen Christ as a cosmic figure might also be a reworking of this (see also Ephesians 1:10, 23).

4 Jewish myths

KEY ISSUE Myths in the Jewish Bible (the Christian Old Testament) are reworked Ancient Near Eastern myths, chiefly from Babylon and Canaan.

a) The chaos myth

Canaanite myths, and the Babylonian story of creation, reveal the idea that chaos was the natural state of things. There was a cosmic struggle in the beginning, to bring order out of chaos, and this is an ongoing struggle which ritual and sacrifice sustains. In the Ba'al stories, this is tied in with the dying/rising god idea. Chaos is often symbolised as a dragon, the devouring Tiamat in Babylonian lore, and as raging waters, Yamm, in Canaanite sources. These themes recur in the Old Testament, as in the use of chaos in the first creation story in Genesis 1:1, where the 'deep' (*tehom*) is a version of the Babylonian Tiamat. The dragon and the waters are mentioned in Isaiah 51:9–10:

> Was it not you who cut Rahab in pieces, who pierced the dragon? Was it not you who dried up the sea [yam], the waters of the great deep [tehom]; who made the depths of the sea a way for the redeemed to cross over?

This passage uses chaos monster images for the **Exodus**, not the Creation, for this refers to crossing the Sea of Reeds to escape from the Egyptians.

When we come to the New Testament, these themes recur. Christ stills the storm, walks on water, and defeats the dragon, Satan:

> The great dragon was thrown down, the ancient serpent, who is called the Devil and Satan, the deceiver of the whole world ...
>
> Revelation 12:9

The Resurrection is a new creation, overcoming the forces of chaos.

b) The end times

The Ancient Near Eastern myths were cyclical and seasonal. The Old Testament refashioned these into a historical drama. God acted at various points to overcome the forces of evil and to lead his people on, as in the Exodus. The prophets spoke of a final blessing, a final struggle when all would be renewed (as in Isaiah 11:6–9; 2). Jewish sages and poets cast this hope into vivid poetry at the time of Jesus, called **apocalyptic** (see page 16). The defeat of the dragon, the defeat of the waters, and of death itself were on the horizon. A key element in this mythology is the sacred mountain. Ancient Near Eastern myths had a secret place, a navel of the earth, the primal mountain where creation began. This was the special dwelling or gateway to the gods, where a temple was built. Ba'al had Mt Zaphon, Marduk had Babylon, and **Yahweh** had first Sinai, and later Zion (Jerusalem). In pagan religions the mountain was a symbol of security and order. It was this too in the Old Testament, for this was the place from which Yahweh reigned, but it was also a place of final blessing, of end-time fulfilment. Thus Isaiah 25:7-8a says:

> And he will destroy on this mountain the shroud that is cast over all peoples, the sheet that is spread over all nations; he will swallow up death for ever.

Jesus gives the new law in the Sermon on the Mount; he is transfigured on a mountain; he commissions his disciples on a mountain. He is even crucified on the mountain of Calvary. The final passages of the book of Revelation see a reworking of the mountain imagery, as all nations are blessed by the presence of God and the Lamb – the whole creation is as the holy mountain, the New Jerusalem (Revelation 21).

5 The Jesus myth

KEY ISSUE Jewish thought introduced the concept of salvation history, the idea that history is going somewhere. It has a goal. The New Testament writers saw this goal in Christ – he is the defeat of chaos and the renewal of all things.

It is really in the difference in New Testament mythology that we see creative insight. The Hellenistic world knew of no exact parallel to the idea of incarnation, that God could really take flesh. They knew appearance, disguise, inspiration and blessing, but not incarnation. Jewish thought spoke of God being intertwined in human life, passionately involved through his Spirit, Wisdom or Word, seen as extensions of his being, but it stopped short of incarnation. A God who suffered was a crazy idea to a Greek, and a God in human form was a dangerous nonsense to the Jew. Thus Paul can say in 1 Corinthians 1:23:

> '...but we proclaim Christ crucified, a stumbling block to Jews and foolishness to Gentiles'.

The New Testament reworks ancient, mythological themes but a problem remains. The significance of Jesus, his person, his goal, his Resurrection and return might all be coloured by and dressed up in mythological garb, but what really do these stories point to? A religious myth might be about God doing something, but what if this action is located in a specific time in history, in a specific man, and not in the eternity of heaven? Thus, the Exodus was an event, something happened to the waters and the Hebrews fled to safety. The interpretation is mythical, as in the Isaiah passage above, and needs to be if the event is not to be a bare event – it is salvation history, spiritually charged and of epic significance.

When faced with New Testament myths, scholarship has tended to go in two distinct directions. The first is that of the **demythologising**, or **existential** school. The second affirms that God acts in history, though we need to express this in mythological stories and symbols. This is sometimes called remythologising.

a) Demythologising

This was pioneered by the German scholar Rudolf Bultmann in 1941. He tried to highlight how different the NT worldview was from the modern one – a three-decker universe (heaven/earth/hell) with angels, demons, and supernatural causes of what we would now call natural events (e.g. demon possession = madness):

> It is no longer possible for anyone seriously to hold the New Testament view of the world.
>
> *Theology of the New Testament*, p. 4

He sought to interpret the old myths in the terms of existential philosophy, influenced by the work of Heidegger. The myths tell us about inner truths. The cross is about forgiveness and dying to selfish concerns; the Resurrection about new life and hope within.

> To believe in the cross of Christ does not mean to concern ourselves with a mythical process wrought outside of us and our world, or with an objective event turned by God to our advantage, but rather to make the cross of Christ our own, to undergo crucifixion with him.
>
> *Theology of the New Testament*, p. 36

> The real Easter faith is faith in the word of preaching which brings illumination.
>
> *Theology of the New Testament*, p. 42

The cosmic conflict is thus made into an inner truth, a psychodrama; our pride and ruthless ambition can be sacrificed and humbled, being turned into grace and service. Many object that this reduces theology to psychology or anthropology, and this is not without some justification. To be fair to Bultmann, though, he believed in God's reality. In Jesus he saw the definitive revelation of God's grace, his utter forgiveness, but what really matters is what happens inside us.

b) Remythologising

Reactions to Bultmann came from his own pupils, such as Ernst Kasemann in 1953. He retorted that the Gospels are narratives and not abstract philosophy or even psychology. The acts of God are reported, albeit in mythological garb. The Gospel is about something *outside of us* before it is apprehended *within*. Perhaps New Testament theology is about an inseparable, two-sided coin – divine actions out there and the working of inward grace in the believer. The New Testament myths are about spiritual as well as existential realities. When speaking of the activity of the divine, the Beyond, we have to use myth. However we might seek to interpret these in modern terms, we cannot do without them. The myths are not useless old husks from which to extract kernels of truth. They are alive and active today.

Take demon possession, for example. Might this not come alive, not literally as belief in nasty beings that get into some person's mind, but as a first century insight that the problems besetting people are deep, tangled and spiritual, as well as psychological? Are we too bland in our analysis of people today in terms of repressed emotions and traumas? Jung felt the need for myth and symbol to express the inexpressible. There might be depths to the human psyche that we are only dimly aware of.

The Devil, too, is a potent symbol of the mystery and power of evil, not only within each one of us, but existing as a force, a tradition, in its own right *beyond* us. Where it ultimately comes from is a mystery, perhaps from our accumulated evil actions, perhaps even beyond these. The myth of the Devil as a fallen angel affirms that evil is not part of God's purpose. It is rebellion, corruption, turning away from the good. The Resurrection might use the stage craft of ancient myth and bright lights, voices, and angels, but it affirms that Jesus rose, and is mysteriously alive beyond the grave. Also, with miracle stories, we might be dealing with paranormal forces that are only just being discovered. We cannot assume, so confidently, that all such tales of supernatural intervention are purely symbolic. The mind might have peculiar influences over the body, the power of faith does sometimes cure, and nature unfolds itself as ever more amazing.

Alien though some of the New Testament world might seem, it engages the human condition, and faces us with universal questions that exercise our thoughts today as much as then:

- What is God?
- How can people find peace with God?
- What happens after death?
- What is the 'good life'?

Studying the New Testament makes one grapple with Jesus of Nazareth. How much of the traditions can be trusted? Is there an original, accurate portrait of Jesus under the later legends? Did he work miracles, and was God in him? The Gospels present many challenges. There is something enigmatic about Jesus, whatever our beliefs. In the words of a New Testament scholar from earlier in the twentieth century, Albert Schweitzer:

> He comes to us as One unknown, without a name, as of old, by the lakeside. He came to those men who knew him not ... He will reveal Himself in the toils, the conflicts, the sufferings which they shall pass through in His fellowship, and as an ineffable mystery, they shall learn in their own experience Who he is.
>
> *The Quest of the Historical Jesus*, p. 401

Summary List

- Myths are deeply symbolic stories containing important philosophical and spiritual insights.
- God and the spiritual dimension of life need to be expressed in mythological terms, for they are beyond everyday language and

perception. We use symbol, story, analogy and imagination to express that which cannot be expressed otherwise.

- The Bible is often based upon historical facts and incidents, such as the life of Jesus or the Exodus from Egypt. The reportage of bare facts needs to be dressed up in mythological imagery to get across spiritual content.
- The OT reworks earlier Canaanite myths to put a new spiritual spin on them – chaos is checked at the Creation and will be defeated one day at the coming of the Kingdom of God. The sacred mountain also figures, as in Sinai.
- The NT picks up the OT themes and builds on them. Christ walking on water suggests defeating chaos; teaching and being transfigured on a mountain suggests revealing God on the sacred mount.
- Hellenistic myths also come into play and are used in the NT – the demigod wonder worker; the rewarding of a virtuous man with immortality. The evangelists use the thought-forms of their day, but twist these around to reveal new insights. Jesus was not half-human but fully human. God did not appear to come on earth, but actually took flesh.
- Modern readers of the NT need to be conscious of the mythical content, but there are two approaches to this:
  – Demythologising tries to strip myth away and re-express this in terms of existentialist philosophy. Faith is about something inside us.
  – Remythologising admits the need for mythological language to express spiritual truths that cannot be reduced to human concerns and experience. A fundamental mystery lies behind the symbolic material. Faith is about something that happens outside us and affects us on the inside.

Answering structured and essay questions on Chapter 1

Studying ancient texts, customs and beliefs such as the New Testament cannot help but raise questions for today. Not only do modern believers regard the New Testament as a living book, i.e. a book that is relevant for today, but any human being has thoughts, questions and feelings about religious truth. Think about the following questions:

1. What ideas about God do you have, and how do these compare with Christian ideas about God?
   (Jesus revealed God as a compassionate Father, as well as the cosmic Lord. In the Gospel stories, God comes down to earth, gets involved in the creation, acting as a servant to reach out to people and offer forgiveness. God 'suffered and bled' in the man Jesus.)
2. How can people find peace with God?
   (Different religions set out ways of worshipping God, and codes to live by. The NT presents many moral ideas, but the central theme is grace.

Grace can be defined as 'unmerited favour'. Though people do not deserve love and forgiveness, God offers it to all. This is seen supremely on the cross.)

3. What do you think happens after death, and how does this compare with Christian beliefs?
(The NT presents the belief in resurrection, or the 'life of the world to come'. This cannot be described as it is a mystery, but the Resurrection of Jesus is a sign and a pledge of that new life.)
4. What moral and spiritual challenges does the Christian myth give to modern society?
(Christians see human beings as not just the product of blind evolution, but as the purposeful plan of a loving God.)
5. Read the following passages and then suggest the mythological themes that might be present from OT or Hellenistic sources: Matthew 5:1–2; Matthew 8:1–13; Mark 4:35–41; Mark 6:45–52.
6. **a)** What is meant by demythologising?
b) How would you demythologise a passage like Matthew 28:1–10?
c) What is meant by remythologising?
d) How would a remythologiser interpret Matthew 28:1–10?
7. 'Human kind cannot bear very much reality' T. S. Eliot. Is myth merely a distraction, or a way of expressing great themes and truths? Include material from the Bible and use contemporary examples from the media.

2 What is the New Testament?

KEYWORDS

apocalyptic – ideas about the end of the world, expressed in vivid poetry

discourse – lengthy speeches containing theological teaching

epiphany – an appearance of God's presence and power

Epistle – a letter written to an early Christian Church

exorcism – casting out evil spirits

eschatology – the end time, the end of the world

Gospel – literally 'good news' book, about the life of Jesus

Gnosticism – movement that sought mystical knowledge (*gnosis*) to find God

Jesus tradition – the oral tradition passed down by the early Christians about Jesus

logia – 'sayings', the sayings of Jesus written down

parable – a story containing a spiritual truth

parousia – literally 'presence', the Second Coming of Christ

pseudopigraphy – works written by a disciple but attributed to his master

1 Content

KEY ISSUE The Christian Bible is made up of two sections: the Old Testament and the New Testament. 'Testament', or 'covenant', means a special promise. The OT is based upon Moses giving the Law at Mount Sinai; the NT is based upon the life, death and Resurrection of Jesus.

The New Testament is made up of twenty-seven books: four **Gospels**; the Acts of the Apostles (telling the early history of the Church); twentyone **Epistles**, or letters; and the Apocalypse, or Book of Revelation (which tells of the coming of the Kingdom of God in vivid poetry and symbols).

a) The Gospels

The four Gospels of Matthew, Mark, Luke and John are 'good news' books (from the Greek *euanggelion*, 'good news'). These preach the message of Jesus of Nazareth, who is proclaimed as the promised Messiah. They are reflections upon the life of Jesus which assume belief in his Resurrection. That belief colours everything that was received in the '**Jesus tradition**': the material handed down as being said or done by him.

The Gospels mainly tell about the last few years of Jesus' life, and concentrate on his final week. Mark, for example, uses nearly five of his sixteen chapters to deal with this. It is thought likely that the Passion narrative, detailing the events of Jesus' last week and the journey to the cross, was the earliest section of the Gospel story to be written This might have been for apologetic reasons, as Jeremias has suggested, to show the Romans that Jesus was not a criminal. It might also have been for liturgical use, as the Church gathered to celebrate the Eucharist (see 1 Corinthians 11:23–25 where Paul quotes a section of the Passion Narrative in such a context).

Other stories and sayings of Jesus were probably handed down in topical collections, either in written or oral form (see, for example, Mark 1:21–3:12 where there is a series of 'wonder stories' of healing miracles or **exorcisms**; or Mark 4:1–31, where there is a collection of sayings and **parables**). Mark is thought to be the earliest Gospel; and Matthew and Luke follow his material and order very closely. Much of their additional material is in common, and this is referred to by scholars as 'Q', short for 'Quelle' (German: 'source'). It is debated whether this was a written or an oral source, and whether it was material gathered by either Matthew or Luke and used by the other. John is very different in structure and in the order of events. He is thought to use different traditions.

Another feature to be noted in the study of the Gospels is that of the literary genres used. Miracle stories, for example, follow a literary pattern found in the writings of the ancient world. The genre of **epiphany** (a manifestation of a divine being or power) is also present, utilising bright light, heavenly voices, and a feeling of dread and awe (e.g. the transfiguration story in Mark 9:1–8). This genre is frequently found in the Hellenistic myths about the gods. A good example is the birth of Dionysus, whose mother was made pregnant by Zeus. One version of the story says that she asked to see Zeus in his real form, without any human disguise. He appeared in fierce and shining light, so that the mortal woman shrivelled up and died. Other versions suggest Zeus struck her down with a thunderbolt for denying that she was pregnant by him. The poet Euripides refers to this (in the *Bacchae*) as follows:

> **Dionysus:** I am Dionysus, son of Zeus. My mother was Semele, Cadmus' daughter. From her womb the fire of a lightning flash delivered me... Here her house stood: and its ruins smoulder with the still living flame of Zeus' fire …

The experience of awe and fear in the presence of someone who reveals his divinity is also a feature of epiphany, besides a shining light, and so at the end of the *Bacchae*, Dionysus is revealed:

> **Chorus:** But look! Who is this, rising above the palace door? It is he – Dionysus comes himself, no more disguised as mortal, but in the glory of his divinity!
> **Dionysus:** Behold me, a god great and powerful...
> **Cadmus:** Have mercy on us, Dionysus. We have sinned.

Compare the Gospel accounts of the transfiguration to see if these same features are present. What do you think the cloud suggests? (Note OT examples, e.g. Exodus 16:10; Isaiah 6:1–5.)

b) The Acts of the Apostles

Acts is the second volume of Luke, telling the story from the Ascension of Christ until the imprisonment of Paul in Rome. It tells the story of the early Jerusalem Church in a series of swift scenes in chapters 1–12; and having introduced Saul/Paul, his missionary journeys become the focus in chapters 13–28. The author may have been a travelling companion of Paul (see the 'we' passages, e.g. 20:5–16), or a later author might have used an ancient travel diary as a source.

c) The Epistles

These were letters written by the apostles, or their later followers, sending advice to the church communities they had founded or had some other connection with. These contain teaching about Christian doctrine, they show how the early Christians used the Old Testament, and they give glimpses of the social life and organisation of the early churches. First century writers often practised **pseudopigraphy**, works they attributed to another person. This was not lying, but an act of respect and dedication. Some of the Epistles that claim to come from Paul might be from later Christians who were his disciples, carrying on his ideas. Some Epistles are definitely from Paul – Romans, 1 and 2 Corinthians, Galatians. Scholars have different ideas about the authorship of the rest.

d) Revelation

This final book of the New Testament is concerned with **eschatology**: the 'last things', the 'end time'. It is **apocalyptic** literature because it 'reveals' the last things. It was written in a time of persecution, and contrasts the sufferings and trials of the Church at that time with the glories of the age to come. It prophesies the second coming of Christ which brings the Kingdom of God to earth, a doctrine known as the ***parousia***, (Greek: 'the presence' or 'arrival of a ruler at his court'). The earliest Christians preached an imminent *parousia*, e.g. Peter in Acts 2:14–40 and Paul in 2 Thessalonians 2. The fact that this did not happen caused much soul-searching in early Christianity. The turning point was AD 70 when Jerusalem was destroyed. (This seems to have been hinted at by Jesus in Mark 13; Luke 21; Matthew 24–25; see especially Luke 21:20–21.) Yet, the Kingdom did not come. Luke works with a theology of the age of the Church and the Spirit, in between the age of Jesus and the *parousia*. The theme of Acts is how the Spirit calls people to repent and join the Church, before the end comes.

2 Dating the Gospels

KEY ISSUE The names of the four Gospels are only traditional: they do not form a part of the original text. There is widespread debate about who actually wrote the Gospels, and when.

It might be that the apostles or the early Christians after whom the Gospels were named had some connection with the material. So Matthew might have compiled a collection of sayings of Jesus (known as **logia**) or of OT proof texts (showing how Jesus had fulfilled them). The tradition of the teaching of Papias, bishop of Hierapolis *c.* AD 130, states that 'Mark was the interpreter of Peter', and that Matthew wrote the sayings 'in the Hebrew language'. Papias also suggests that there was a living oral tradition in his day, well after the time when the Gospels were written:

> I supposed that things out of books did not profit me so much as the utterances of a voice which lives and abides.

Certainly the Gospels were written by the end of the first century because second century Christian writers such as Papias and Irenaeus mention them. Also, some of the words of Jesus from the Sermon on the Mount in Matthew were reproduced by Clement of Rome in his first Epistle (*c.* AD 95) and were regarded as having the same authority as verses of the Old Testament Scripture. (He does not, however, tell us that there was a written Gospel; he might have received these logia from oral tradition.) The early Christians adopted the codex, the book form, from the Romans, rather than follow the Jewish custom of having a scroll for their Scriptures. This was probably because a codex could contain all four Gospels at once. The practice of copying only four of the many Gospels available seems to have been adopted quite early, possibly by the second century AD, following evidence of codex fragments from collections in Oxford, Barcelona and Paris.

Finally, the earliest fragment of John is dated AD 110–150, and was found in the sands of Egypt. Allowing sufficient time for it to have been copied, circulated, and to have gained authority as a valid Gospel, John is usually dated *c.* AD 95. The suggested dates for the Gospels are only speculative; the Gospels might contain much earlier written material that the evangelists used.

There are other fragments that are claimed by some to be even earlier, though the scholarly world is divided. Two fragments of Matthew 26, kept at Magdalen College, Oxford, are widely thought to date from the late second century. Some scholars, such as Carsten Thiede, argue for a first century date. Even more debatable is a fragment from one of the Qumran caves, among the Dead Sea Scrolls. This fragment is claimed by some to be part of Mark 6. If genuine, this would date this Gospel to a time pre-AD 70 when the documents were hidden.

The issue of the date of the Gospels was opened up in the 1970s by John Robinson's *Redating the New Testament.* His arguments can be complicated and, though the book is worth dipping into, you will find a clear summary of his position in his shorter title *Can we trust the New Testament?* He argues that there is no mention of AD 70 and the fall of the Temple anywhere in the NT and that such a major event would have warranted a mention in the Gospels or Epistles. The apocalyptic passages of the teaching of Jesus (Mark 13, Matthew 24–25) are interesting in this regard since they do not mention the fall of the city or Temple, though they predict there will be a general catastrophe. Luke 21:20 is more explicit. Jerusalem will be surrounded by armies. Still, for Robinson, this is just a general description of warfare and not the account of AD 70 in particular, or it might be a later addition, a form of 'prophecy after the event'. John 2:19 might also contain a veiled reference to the destruction of the Temple: 'Destroy this temple, and in three days I will raise it up'. Robinson's argument is not conclusive, as with any argument based on silence.

3 Only four Gospels?

KEY ISSUE There are four Gospels in the canon of the New Testament. There were other gospels written, though, which the early Church decided not to include in he official canon of Scriptures.

Most of these other gospels were late compositions from the second century AD, and contain legendary material. They are more fantastic, with exaggerated miracle stories. So, the child Christ walks on a sunbeam or makes a clay bird come to life, or his infancy is expanded and all sorts of spurious details are added.

a) *The Gospel of Peter*

Only 60 verses survive, which retell the Passion and Resurrection very closely to the New Testament accounts. However, some details are added. The actual Resurrection is witnessed by the soldiers, who see three men coming out of the tomb, with a cross following them. Jesus, when on the cross, is described as being 'silent, having no pain'. This suggests that the Gospel was later, adding legendary details and having a more unrealistic idea of Jesus.

b) *The Egerton Gospel*

This is named after four fragments called Papyrus Egerton 2, found in Egypt. Most of the material is similar to the canonical Gospels, though one section is a fanciful account of the infancy of Christ.

c) *The Secret Gospel of Mark*

This is a controversial piece, discovered in 1958 by Morton Smith, and published in 1973. He claims to have discovered a previously unknown letter of Clement of Alexandria, writing in about AD 200. Clement mentions passages from a secret gospel, which Mark had also produced, for more advanced disciples. This contains an enigmatic passage where a young man visits Jesus by night naked except for a linen robe. Hints of an inner circle and initiation rites suggest that this was a heretical work, and some have accused Morton Smith of forgery, as he has never produced the original manuscript for comparative study.

d) The Gnostic Gospels

Gnosticism was a religious movement that flourished in the second century AD, but might have had its origins in the first century. Gnostics believed that the world was evil, and that secret knowledge was given to an initiate to escape to a purer world. Sparks of divine light were in each person, and the soul could be guided back to God through different levels, with angels as guides. There were varieties of Gnostic belief, all stressing inner wisdom and enlightenment. There was a Gnostic movement among the early Christians, with Jesus as the Revealer of the way back to God, but they denied that he actually took flesh and suffered on the cross (this belief is also known as Docetism, from *dokeo* in Greek, meaning to appear or to seem, because it only seemed that Jesus suffered). The Gnostics produced a number of gospels, presenting their ideas on the lips of Jesus, with titles such as the Gospel of Truth, or the Gospel of Mary.

e) *The Gospel of Thomas*

This is the most interesting of the non-canonical, or apocryphal gospels. The form discovered at Nag Hammadi in Egypt has Gnostic features. It opens with the claim that 'these are the secret sayings which Jesus uttered ...' and the other documents found with the gospel were Gnostic. However, a number of scholars feel that there could be a more primitive *Gospel of Thomas* under this Gnostic editing. Most of the gospel is a series of logia, and some are paralleled in the New Testament. Some of the Thomas versions are simpler and shorter, suggesting that they might be more primitive. So, for example, Thomas's version of the Parable of the Sower (which you can compare with Mark 4:3-8):

> Jesus said, 'Listen, a sower came forth, took a handful, and scattered. Now some fell upon the path, and the birds came and picked them out. Others fell upon the rock, and they did not take root in the soil, and they did not send up ears. Others fell on thorns, and they choked the seed; and the grubs devoured them. And others fell upon good soil, and it produced a good crop: it yielded sixty per measure and a hundred and twenty per measure ...'
>
> logion 9

Thomas might have been a collection of early sayings, as with Q. As such, it has been included in a controversial book, *The Five Gospels* by a group of radical US scholars, the Jesus Seminar. It is accorded equal weight with the four Gospels, and the Seminar members vote on which logia they think were authentic sayings of the historical Jesus. Their results are interesting, but quite extreme.

f) The Jewish-Christian Gospels

Fragments survive of gospels composed by Jewish-Christian groups who kept close to the primitive Jerusalem traditions and followed the Torah. These gospels emphasise social responsibility more, so that one can say:

> And never be joyful except when you look on your brother with love.
>
> *Hebrews*, fragment 5

i) The Gospel of the Nazarenes
This is a later version of Matthew, an imaginative expansion of many of its logia and episodes (e.g. the man with the withered hand is a builder who wants to be healed to carry on his work, and the garments of the magi are described in detail).

ii) The Gospel of the Ebionites
This was composed by a group in Trans-Jordan, and is a reworking of Matthew, with some material from Mark and Luke. It makes significant alterations:

- Rejection of the virgin birth
- Vegetarianism, so that John the Baptist eats only honey (not locusts)
- Rejection of the Temple cult. Jesus says, 'I am come to do away with sacrifices, and if you do not cease from sacrificing, the wrath of God will not cease from you'.

fragment 6

iii) The Gospel of the Hebrews
A lengthy work, known only from seven fragments, and quoted by writers such as Origen and Clement of Alexandria. It seems to have been inspired by Gnosticism, though it is still very Jewish. Much is made of the appearance of the risen Christ to James (fleshing out 1 Corinthians 15:7) and the Holy Spirit is feminine (from the Semitic word *ruach* for spirit, which is feminine in form) Jesus says,

> Even so did my mother, the Holy Spirit, take me by one of my hairs and carry me away on to the great mountain Tabor.

Gnostic influence can be seen in the various stages of revelation or salvation that the soul goes through, and even the Holy Spirit finds rest by filling the pre-existent Son at the baptism! This influence is sketchy, though, for so little remains of the gospel. It might be an early form of proto-Gnostic spirituality that was earthed in Judaism.

Summary List

a) Date chart

BC

c. 6	birth of Jesus

AD

c. 27/28	Jesus' baptism
c. 30/33	Jesus' crucifixion
c. 36	Saul's conversion
50	Council of Jerusalem (Acts 15)
48–65	Paul's Epistles

62	martyrdom of James
65-66	Nero's persecution in Rome (when Peter and Paul probably died)
c. 65/70	Mark written
66–70	Jewish War
70	fall of Jerusalem
85	Council of Jamnia (Jewish Christians regarded as heretics)
85–90(?)	Luke and Matthew written
c. 95(?)	John written

b) The Bible

- It is in two sections or 'covenants'/'testaments'.
- The NT contains a variety of writings: Gospels, Epistles, an apocalyptic book about the end of the world, and Acts about the early Church.
- The Gospels were all written by the end of the first century AD, drawing upon earlier oral and (possibly) written collections of logia – sayings of Jesus.
- The NT uses recognised literary genres of the time, such as epiphany and miracle to express spiritual truth.
- Later gospels from the second century AD were not included in the canon of Scripture as these were more legendary, or were influenced by heretical groups such as the Gnostics and Ebionites. There is some interesting material in these, though, and there might be primitive, reliable material here and there, as in *Thomas*.

Answering structured and essay questions on Chapter 2

1. Read Philemon, a brief example of an Epistle. Note any stylised, standard literary devices as in the introduction and conclusion. What teaching about Christ and about how a Christian should live are to be found in this document?
2. Read Revelation 5 and list any symbols that can be found there. What does this say about Christ?
3. Say which genres the following passages belong to: Matthew 1:1–17; Mark 2:1–11; Mark 4:1–9; Mark 5:1–20; Matthew 5:1–12; Mark 9:2–8; Mark 13:24–27; Mark 15.
4. Ebionites and Gnostics – why were their Gospels rejected?

3 The Hellenistic World

KEYWORDS

demiurge – a go-between deity, creating the world for the High God

'divine men' – demigods, half human and half gods. Wise men or heroes who were thought to be the offspring of a god and a woman, or were empowered by the gods

euanggelion – 'good news'

mysteries – secret rites to try to find immortality

Pax Romana – the Roman peace, as the legions kept control of the Empire

Platonists – followers of the philosopher Plato

pleroma – fullness

Stoics – they believed that the logos (reason) was in all living beings

1 The power of Rome

Jesus was born into a world ruled by Rome, under the Emperor Augustus. Rome was once just a powerful city in Italy, until it conquered neighbouring states and ruled the land. Then it slowly built up an empire, conquering Carthage in North Africa, and controlling the Mediterranean. The Greek nations came under Roman rule and Rome inherited the learning of the Greeks. Augustus had put an end to civil war in Rome and established the ***Pax Romana***, the peace that spread from Britain in the West to the River Euphrates in the East. The Roman legions ensured that a traveller could freely pass, unmolested, from one end of the empire to the other. There was a common language, Greek; this was known in the East and West, because of the great Greek writers and philosophers.

The next four rulers after Augustus were all related to him: Tiberius, Caligula, Claudius and Nero. After this, because of Nero's unpopularity, popular generals were chosen as emperor. Trajan was the last emperor in the first century AD, closing the New Testament period.

2 The ruler cult

The cult of the divine ruler came from Egypt and Babylon. Alexander had used it to his advantage in Egypt, calling himself the son of Zeus, and the Roman Emperors from Julius Caesar onwards were to be hailed with divine titles. Caesar was known as 'offspring of Ares and Aphrodite, and common saviour of human life'. Augustus was known as god and lord. An emperor's visit could be referred to as a *parousia* or as an epiphany (arrival, or appearance/manifestation of the divine). The ruler cult was used later to ensure loyalty among the subjects, and the Christians were faced with the choice of sacrificing to Caesar as Lord, or being faithful to Jesus as Lord. The role of the cult in earlier times is vaguer, and does not seem to have been a challenge to the first Christians. (Nero's persecution in AD 65–66 was a cover for his engineering the fire of Rome.) It is not clear how often prayers were offered to the ruler when dead. Some of the titles used of the rulers clearly influenced those used of Jesus such as Lord, Saviour, Son of God. Also, *parousia* and ***euanggelion*** were used of the emperors. One inscription says that the birth of Augustus was 'euanggelion' for the world.

3 The divine men

KEY ISSUE The Hellenistic world told stories of '**divine men**' (*theioi andres*) who were inspired philosophers, powerful rulers, or who worked miracles of healing.

There were stories of healings, miraculous disappearances at death, appearances beyond the grave, and so forth. These men were a race between men and gods, either because they were born as a result of sexual relations between a mortal and a god, or because the gods inspired them with great strength or wisdom. Some worthy men were taken to the gods at their deaths as a reward. The old myths were used in this way by the philosophers. The **Stoics** believed that God was a universal reason in all minds and things; if people lived in harmony with this reason, then they would be happy, and at peace. The myth of Hercules was about the struggles of the perfect man to overcome evil and to bring peace to the world. Others thought the gods mentioned in the old myths, especially in Homer, were originally outstanding men who had become immortal by the power of Zeus (god) who was the father of all. The emperors were honoured in this way along with contemporary miracle workers and teachers. Mark presents Jesus against this background, showing him as a wonder worker, but also as the power and Wisdom of God at work, supremely in the crucifixion (see Mark 15:39), an idea far from any of the Hellenistic stories which were obsessed with power, success and glory.

Augustus Caesar as 'Lord' and 'God' ('Kyrios' and 'Theos')

4 The philosophers

KEY ISSUE The Greeks had developed schools of philosophy where the meaning of the universe, the ideal form of society, and the secrets of the natural world were discussed.

Plato formed the most influential school in the 5th–4th century BC, following on from his master Socrates. He taught that there was an ideal world behind the visible world: so there might be many forms of chairs, but one ideal 'type'. The human soul was the reason, which survived death and joined the universal Reason that guided all things. Aristotle, in the fourth century BC, wrote on many subjects, declaring that all people possess the desire to know. He wrote chiefly about ethics, metaphysics and politics. Again, he believed in the power of the reason over the body, the happy man being he who acquired wisdom and knowledge and lived by it.

The Hellenistic world was moving towards monotheism from the earlier more primitive polytheism of Homer. A concept of the High or One God permeated the writings of the philosophers. In the fifth century BC Xenophanes had written:

> There is one God, always still and at rest, who moves all things with the thoughts of his mind.

Pythagoras taught the oneness of God, and stressed his immanence within creation – God was not just 'out there'. The other gods were either seen as aspects of God or as holy, wise, inspired people after their deaths ; and initiates into the **mysteries** could be called 'gods'. We even see a Father/Son language being used of the High God and the immanent God (the Logos). The Logos was the primal thought, through whom all things were made. Heraclitus, in the sixth century BC, had said: 'The Father and the Son are the same'.

The debates and teachings of the philosophers influenced Judaism at the time of Christ. Josephus wrote his *Antiquities of the Jews* to show how Moses and the prophets of the Old Testament were like the philosophers and how cultured a race the Jews were. Philo of Alexandria was a Jewish philosopher who held many of the philosophical ideas of his day such as the Logos (Greek-word/reason) of the **Platonists** and the Stoics. The Stoics believed that a spark of the universal Logos was in every person's soul (see John 1:4).

5 The mystery religions

KEY ISSUE Certain of the gods and goddesses had secret rites attached to their worship; people initiated into these 'mysteries' were bound in a special relationship to the deity, being promised immortality and special favours in this life. Parts of the sanctuaries of the temples of these deities were underground, and it is here that initiations might have taken place. Very little is known of what occurred, for the rites were kept secret.

a) Initiation

Some idea of initiation into the Isis cult is contained in the second century novel *The Golden Ass* (OUP) by Apuleius. The hero, Lucius, is told that once he has been initiated into the mysteries of Isis, he will no longer fear blind fate, but will be under the protection of a goddess who is not blind, but who cares for him. He fasted from meat and wine for ten days, and then had a ritual bath. At night, he passed into the innermost part of the temple, and then the ceremony (which he does not describe) took place. He says it was like entering the underworld and being reborn. He was then set up on a pillar, clothed in a fine robe, with a crown of white palm leaves, and a burning torch in his hand. The others honoured him as a god.

The early philosophers, the founding fathers of rational thought, were initiates into the mysteries, and were bound up with mysticism and intuition. Pythagoras behaved like the leader of a religious cult, practised a form of monasticism, and acted like a guru, performing cures. Plato was inspired by the mysteries and believed in inspiration. He claimed:

> We beheld calm, happy, simple, eternal visions, resplendent in pure light.
>
> *Phaedo*, 250 BC

b) Death and resurrection

The dying and rising god-man was really one person with many names – Mithras, Dionysus, Attis, Osiris, to name but a few, as each region named him differently. He was a deity who appeared briefly in human form as a disguise, and was put to death and then raised up. Some forms of the myth even had the god-man being put to death on a tree. Ancient pictures of the birth of Dionysus have a tree being shown to him, prefiguring his later death, rather like Christian icons of the Christ child seeing a cross held by an angel in the corner. The tree was a fertility symbol, but was associated with crucifixion by some in the ancient world. The god-men had their own passion stories that could be dramatised. In Euripides' *Bacchae*, for example, when Dionysus is arrested by the troops of King Pentheus, he does not resist but offers himself humbly, saying: 'You do not know what you are saying, what you do, nor who you are'.

How 'real' the death of the god-man was is a moot point, for sometimes a substitute died in his place, as in the *Bacchae*. Here, in a frenzy, the people hung up Pentheus, believing him to be Dionysus who slipped his bonds and made good his escape. In contrast, the New Testament claims that Christ really suffered and died. Images of gods on trees/crosses have been found on old carvings, seals and graffiti. Some of these have been assumed to be of Christ, but are probably the mystery deities. One famous piece of graffiti shows a man looking at a crucified man with an ass's head. Many assume that this was mocking the Christians, but it might be an image of Dionysus since the ass was a symbol of folly and the lower self in the Mysteries. The god-men were depicted riding on an ass to show that they had conquered their baser, animal nature. Just think how the story of Christ's triumphal entry on a donkey would have appeared to a pagan! True, this was a fulfilment of a Jewish oracle, and an act of deliberate humility, but it was rich in association in the Hellenistic world.

c) Christian parallels

The cross was sometimes used as a symbol in the mysteries as it represented the four seasons, or the four elements of earth, air, fire and water. The rites of initiation could include blood, water, fire, air wafted by fans and being smeared with ashes. A sacred meal was sometimes shared, often of bread and wine. There are obvious parallels with the Christ story. Early Christians rejected the Mysteries as Satanic copies of the true faith, while pagans scoffed that the Christians were really saying nothing new. Perhaps we are dealing with deep mythological structures and collective symbols of the human quest for divine compassion and the nature of atonement. C. S. Lewis went so far as to claim that the old myths were like good dreams given to humanity to prepare them for the birth of Christ, the real historical God-man. The truth is that Dionysus *et al* were all mythical beings. Not one of them ever existed, being symbols of nature and the seasons, whereas Jesus was born in the reign of Tiberius Caesar and crucified under Pontius Pilate.

It is interesting to see what influence these cults had on early Christianity. Much of the language of dying and rising with Christ in baptism (see Romans 6:3–5) can be paralleled with the mystery religions, as can the hope of immortality that followed. There were also very high moral expectations of the initiates as there were of newly-baptised Christians. Above the shrine of Asclepius was the inscription: 'Purity is thinking only holy thoughts'. The Pythagoreans

Graffiti of man worshipping a man on cross with ass's head mocking Christ or an image of a mystery deity

had to search their consciences each night to examine their behaviour, and the Roman Seneca sat up in bed doing just this, offering his lower self forgiveness from his higher self: 'Take care not to repeat them, and also I forgive you today'. At initiation, the priest of the shrine would act as a god-man and would hear the initiates' confessions. Nero withdrew from being an initiate because he knew that he would have to confess to murdering his mother!

Thus we can see how rites, symbols and codes would have been similar to those of early Christianity. When the faith moved from its Jewish roots out into the Hellenistic world it took on forms and language akin to the common thought world of the mysteries. However, Jesus was a real man in history rather than a mythical deity, and the Church was open to all races and classes of society. The mystery cults were elitist, reserved for professionals and soldiers. Though they achieved a certain kind of international brotherhood (initiates were 'brothers' or even *frates carissimos* – most loving brothers) and a levelling of their members, only some people were eligible to join in. It is significant that a number of slaves were attracted to Christianity because it offered them a hope that no one else did.

6 Gnosticism

> **KEY ISSUE** The term 'Gnostic' derives from the Greek word for knowledge, *gnosis*. Gnosticism described a varied group of beliefs that involved the possession of some secret knowledge that made the person wise or offered salvation.

The term 'Gnosticism' is often bandied about in New Testament scholarship, and it is important to understand what might and might not be meant.

Gnosticism proper was a highly developed mythology and philosophical system that flourished in the second century AD onwards. Much of our knowledge of this comes from the Church Fathers, such as Irenaeus, who described Gnostic teaching in order to refute it. Gnostic ideas had become so widespread and popular that Gnostic versions of Christianity were developing that slotted Jesus into the heterodox, largely pagan, scheme. Even from the evidence in the writings of the orthodox Christians, we see that there were wide varieties of belief among the Gnostics, and this was one of the charges brought against them, that they had no coherent message and had rival schools. In 1945, a collection of Gnostic texts was found at Nag Hammadi in Egypt. There were over forty documents, containing some non-Christian texts and Christian ones – the most famous being the *Gospel of Thomas*.

These are Coptic copies of earlier, Greek texts, some dating back to the second century AD. Some of the documents, such as wisdom and philosophical teachings, are not, technically, Gnostic, but were congenial to their position. This collection solves nothing about the origins of Gnosticism, but it affirms what the Church Fathers had to say since these accounts are very faithful to the ideas in the documents. Given that the Fathers could have easily exaggerated the material as it was heresy to them, this is important and interesting.

a) Gnostic characteristics

Gnosticism, despite the varieties of belief, has certain characteristics:

- A radical dualism, of light/dark, good/evil, spirit/matter.
- The material world was seen as the work of a **demiurge**, a lesser god or angel who had fallen into error. The quest for human beings was to allow their souls to escape from the material world and to seek a return to the High God.
- Some systems had elaborate mythologies of levels (aeons) and hierarchies of angels. Valentinian Gnosticism had thirty aeons, forming the ***Pleroma***, the Fullness.

- *Sophia*, Wisdom, is active as a mythological form, or a principle, illuminating the soul. In Valentinus' reworking of the Genesis story, *Sophia* breathes life into Adam, hoping to start a process to free him from matter.
- Christian Gnostics tended to deny or downplay the incarnation – Jesus only appeared to be a man, or he did not actually suffer. In various versions, someone took his place on the cross, or he only appeared to be there, and the enlightened saw him laughing above the gibbet.

The final point about denying the incarnation has to be treated with some caution. There were many different types of Gnostic teaching around this subject. Some followed the mystery cult idea that the deity was the Higher Self, and the embodied person was the Lower Self. The Higher Self was eternal and could not suffer, hence images of Christ laughing in a vision above the cross, for the eternal could not be hurt, only the inferior body he had on earth. Gnostics also played with the concept of twins – the divine Self had an earthly twin, and some spun yarns about a supposed twin brother of Christ, Thomas. In some versions of Gnosticism, the earthly twin was put on the cross, being mistaken for the divine Christ. We can see these kind of ideas behind the teaching in the Muslim holy book, the Qur'an. Muhammad would have had contact with various heterodox groups of Christians. The Qu'ran teaches;

> But they did not kill him, neither did they crucify him, but a similitude was made for them.
>
> *Sura 4:156–157*

Did this mean that a substitute person was crucified, and not Jesus, or does it mean that the eternal part of him could not be hurt? Thus, some of the Gnostics did hold to an actual incarnation of sorts, making sense of Christ's two natures in the mystery-religion fashion of the Higher Self/Lower Self.

Gnostics stressed personal experience and inner enlightenment. They went too far, however, when they taught that they could become Christ. The Gnostic initiates saw themselves as above the authority of the orthodox bishops, whom they accused of leading Psychic Christians, at the very first stages of enlightenment. Even this robust language has echoes in the genuine Jesus tradition (see John 10:34–36 where Jesus allows that people who have received the word of God can be called 'gods'). Clement of Alexandria also called Christian initiates 'gods'. The orthodox stopped short of identification with Christ and God, though – the Christian was subject to Christ as Head of the body.

b) Primal Man and Cosmic Redeemer

One interesting feature in much later Gnosticism is the myth of the Primal Man and the Cosmic Redeemer. The Primal Man was a heavenly being who fell into matter, and was broken up and scattered into thousands of souls. Each person thus contains a divine spark within. The Cosmic Redeemer was another heavenly being who descended to try to gather up the sparks. This redeemer might be *Sophia*, or even Jesus in some Christian forms. There is no definite evidence for the existence of these myths until the third century AD with the writings of Manichaeism. Some scholars, such as Bultmann, were convinced that they must have been earlier, and saw the New Testament as an attempt to articulate the Christ event by use of this contemporary myth – it made sense then, a deeply redemptive story about the love and mercy of God coming down to find us and take us home. Did Paul use this with his First Adam/Second Adam imagery in 1 Corinthians 15 ?

c) Origins

The origins of Gnosticism are shrouded in mystery. The second century forms are developed, and there are traces and hints of Gnostic ideas in the first century in the New Testament. Paul's opponents at Corinth seem to have been influenced in this way – the spirit was superior to the material, and it did not matter what you did in the body; and the Resurrection was not an event, but inner illumination. The fourth Gospel has Gnostic echoes about it – light/dark; ascending/descending Son of God; and the Johannine letters stress inner experience of the Spirit as the fount of truth and wise guidance. Yet, the Johannine corpus is orthodox, as it affirms an actual and real incarnation 'in the flesh'. This seems to be the touchstone of orthodoxy for the author(s), for 'antichrist' is described as those who deny that the Son has come in the flesh. Some early texts are on the borderline, and scholars cannot agree whether to call them Gnostic or not. This is the case with the *Odes of Solomon*, a collection of 42 poems which use some Gnostic imagery. They are thought to have originated in the second century AD, some claiming them as orthodox, but mystical, and some seeing them as Gnostic. Also, the writings of Clement of Alexandria use some Gnostic terms within a more orthodox framework. He uses the term *gnosis* quite freely of the Christian initiate. It must be remembered that early Christianity was rather fluid, with different emphases and expressions before it was more regimented and codified in the second century, in response to movements such as Gnosticism. Still, there are common themes and key ideas which distinguish the orthodox, even then, from the heterodox.

Scholars debate the origins of Gnostic ideas. There might have been a cross-referenced, highly fertile soup of ideas in the first century AD, mixing material from Judaism and Hellenism. The Jewish wisdom and apocalyptic traditions began to tend towards mysticism – Philo of Alexandria tried to express the Torah in a thoroughly

Hellenised fashion, of inner illumination and guidance, as the soul took part in the logos (divine reason) that permeated creation. It is not hard to see how apocalyptic writing might have turned inwards, and earth-shaking events were interpreted as inner changes and enlightenment, and fabulous mythologies sprouted about the aeons in the places of all the numerology and dates. Hellenistic culture had a strong undergirding of dualism, stemming from philosophers such as Plato, whereby the soul was trapped in the body like a prison. The mystery cults also had secret knowledge, an initiation into a mystery, that promised immortality. Somehow, somewhere, this syncretism budded and blossomed as Gnosticism, and biblical texts were used, being given Gnostic interpretations, or were reworked, to turn the God of the Old Testament into a demiurge, and the High God was far above the one who soiled his hands making the universe.

d) Conclusions

Popular, racy paperbacks often appear with wild theories about the Gnostics and early Christianity. Some have tried to see the Gnostic gospels as equal in worth to the canonical ones, arguing for an earlier, more philosophical Christianity that was defeated by the orthodox. This is not the view of the scholars, and there is no evidence of the existence of a full-blown Gnostic movement in the first century AD. There is no proof of the existence of a Primal Man/Redeemer myth pre-Christ, either. Developed Gnosticism came later than early Christianity. While some of its ideas were worthy speculations and explorations, stressing the need for inner renewal and experience, its developed form was clearly a deviation from the Jesus tradition.

That is not to deny that there is some valuable material within it, and orthodox Christianity perhaps overreacted in its censure. Any living faith needs an experiential, mystical streak and a dynamic lay spirituality that can operate without always having clergy around. The Gnostics attracted many middle-class Hellenistic women, for their feelings were acknowledged and they could hold positions of authority, acting as priests. The failure of the orthodox to challenge instinctive, institutional sexism in their organisation was a failure to implement the radical teaching of Jesus and the earliest apostolic teaching (see Galatians 3:28). Language of spiritual progress, of going deeper into the mystery of faith, and of Christ as Revealer, should not automatically lead to rejection as Gnostic heresy. In the Gnostic *Pistis Sophia*, for example, the risen Jesus appears to the disciples shining with light. Mary Magdalene says:

> Now we know. O Master, freely, surely, plainly that Thou hast brought the keys of the Mysteries of the Kingdom of Light.

An initiation dance from *The Acts of John* is powerful. The candidate stands before the priest, and the others stand around in a circle. Christ (as the priest) says things like 'I am a lamp to thee who beholdest Me' and 'I am a door to thee who knockest at Me'. And finally, 'Now respond thou to my dancing. See thyself in Me who speaks; and when thou hast seen what I do, keep silence on My mysteries'. Such striking material is usually set in amongst long, complicated genealogies, name lists and bizarre cosmology!

Summary List

- The NT period falls within the *Pax Romana*, when Rome ruled the Mediterranean world.
- The ruler cult had been established, whereby the emperor was hailed as divine and given titles such as 'lord' and 'god'.
- Hellenistic belief in divine men was both mythical (e.g. Heracles) and actual – outstanding warriors, teachers and healers were given this title. They were seen as either specially inspired or honoured by the gods, or as divine offspring of a god and a mortal woman (demigods).
- The Hellenistic world had many different philosophical schools which taught how to live the good life and how to understand truth. The concept of the logos (reason) was highly important.
- Mystery cults flourished as secret fraternities which promised immortality through a series of initiations into the life of a dying and rising god (e.g. Mithras). These were elitist.
- Gnosticism flourished in the second century AD and some early signs of its existence are hinted at in the first century AD. Its origins are unclear, but it seems to have mixed together Jewish esoteric ideas, Hellenistic philosophy and Eastern concepts. In its more advanced forms, it taught that matter was evil and not the world of the High God. Various forms of Christian Gnosticism were around in the second century onwards.

Answering structured and essay questions on Chapter 3

1. How did the *Pax Romana* help the early Church to spread the Gospel?
2. See how many titles and concepts you can trace in Hellenism that occur in the NT.
3. How were the mystery cults similar and dissimilar to Christianity?
4. Who were the Gnostics and why were they condemned as heretics by the early Church?

4 Judaism at the Time of Jesus

KEYWORDS

Essene – member of a separatist group, rejecting the Jerusalem Temple hierarchy

Halakoth – oral teaching about the Torah

Pharisee – one who sought an all-encompassing holiness, with a rich oral tradition of how to interpret the Torah and apply it to everyday life

predestination – belief that God plans the future

Sadducee – landed gentry and traditionalists, only accepting the Torah as Scripture

Sanhedrin – the religious parliament of the Jews in Jerusalem

Septuagint (LXX) – Greek translation of the Hebrew Scriptures

Zealot – one who is zealous for the Torah and prepared to fight in its defence

1 Political background

KEY ISSUE Jesus lived between two periods of liberation struggle by the Jews. The first took place during 169–165 BC, when the Jews defeated the Syrians and won back their independence. The second took place in AD 66–70; but this time the Romans defeated the Jews and destroyed the holy city, Jerusalem. The memory of the earlier victory, and the conviction that the Lord defended the faithful freedom fighters, fuelled common expectations in the period of Roman occupation when Jesus lived.

a) The Maccabees

In 175 BC Antiochus IV Epiphanes ruled in Antioch, and controlled Judaea. He deposed the High Priest, Onias III, and replaced him with Menelaus, who was not of the priestly lineage. Onias was assassinated in 174 BC. A group of Jews, the Hasidim, remained faithful to Onias and were fanatical for the Law, while Antiochus was trying to Hellenise the Jews. It is possible that Onias founded the Qumran community, and was the enigmatic 'Teacher of Righteousness' mentioned in its texts, who was martyred. (The Qumran community was part of a wider movement of people who rejected the Temple hierarchy and its services.) Guerrilla fighting broke out as Jews were forced to eat pork, to work on the Sabbath, and to abandon circumcision. A statue of Zeus was even set up in the Temple. The fighting continued until 165 BC, and was led by Judas 'Maccabaeus' ('the Hammerer'). He won liberty for Judaea, and founded a dynasty, the Hasmoneans. His brothers Jonathan and Simon succeeded him. This period saw the emergence of various religious parties, or sects, such as the **Pharisees**, **Sadducees**, and the **Essenes**.

Jonathan was made the High Priest in 152 BC, by the Syrian king. This ended the hopes of the supporters of Onias for a restored Zadokite priesthood, of the original, priestly line. They retreated to Egypt, where they built a rival Temple at Leontopolis (the Romans destroyed this in AD 73). Jonathan died in 143 BC and his brother Simon was made 'ethnarch' as well as High Priest. His descendent, Aristobulus reigned from 105–104 BC, being the first to use the title 'king'.

b) The Roman occupation

The Hasmonean dynasty was weakened by feuds between the parties of the Pharisees and the Sadducees, and an appeal was made to Rome. The Roman general Pompey marched into Jerusalem in 63 BC. He offended the Jews by looting the treasures from the Temple and entering the holiest part of the shrine, the 'Holy of Holies', where only the High Priest was allowed to go.

The area was ruled by client kings until 4 BC, when Herod the Great died. The area was then divided into four tetrarchies, under Archelaus, Philip, Lysanias, and Herod Antipas. Archelaeus was ruler of Judaea, but he was so unpopular that he was deposed in AD 6 and Judaea was ruled directly by Rome through a prefect. Pontius Pilate was the prefect in AD 26–36. The Jewish leaders had an assembly, the **Sanhedrin**, which decided on religious matters and advised the prefect.

There were a number of Jewish rebellions. The first was in 4 BC after Herod's death. This was the 'Robber War'. According to Josephus, at least two men claimed to be the king of the Jews, one Simon, former slave of Herod's, and also Athronges, a shepherd, who claimed to be the new David. Both men took the royal diadem and proclaimed themselves king. (Josephus writes about them in *Antiquities of the Jews*, 17, 273f and 277–280.) In AD 6, Judas the Galilean led a resistance movement when Judaea and Samaria had been taken under direct Roman rule. He encouraged Jews to stop paying their taxes to Rome, urging the direct rule of God alone. Two of his sons sparked off the same trouble in AD 44 when Galilee came under direct Roman rule. These leaders, and many of their followers, were brutally suppressed, and many were crucified.

c) The Temple at Jerusalem in Herod's day

Herod the Great was an Idumean Arab who had converted to Judaism for political convenience. He was thoroughly Hellenised and unpopular with pious Jews for his laxity with the Law. (He had built a temple to the Emperor Augustus at Sebaste.) He embarked on a massive rebuilding campaign at the Temple. This was the restored Temple (the Second Temple) that had been built by King Solomon and had been partially destroyed by Babylon in the sixth century BC. The returning exiles had rebuilt it, modestly. Herod erected a huge complex of courts and cloisters around the original Temple, creating three courts – one of the Gentiles, one of the Israelite women, and one of the Israelite men. The Temple was within the court of the Israelites. Gentiles were forbidden to move any further in from the outer court on pain of death. An inscription read, 'Let no Gentile enter within this balustrade and enclosure about the holy place and whosoever is caught shall be responsible to himself because death follows.' The outer walls of the Temple were of marble inlaid with gold, and the inner walls were hung with Babylonian tapestries. The door was huge, and the whole edifice was breathtaking.

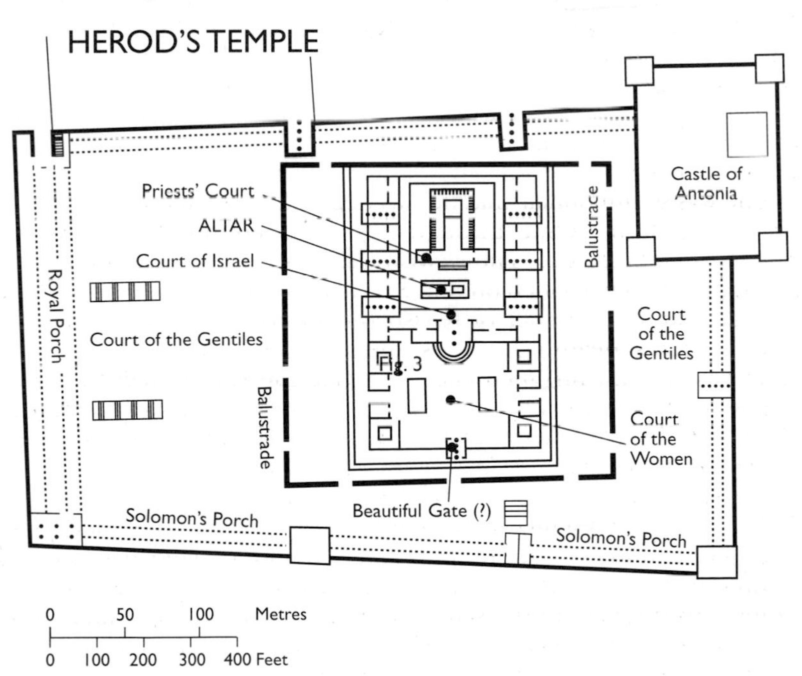

A plan of the Temple. Only the priests were allowed into the Temple proper, and only the High Priest could enter the Holy of Holies, the innermost shrine.

However, a number of pious Jews were ambivalent about the new temple, seeing it as the work of an irreligious ruler, and being far from Solomon's original plan. Some went as far as to distance themselves from the Temple cult (e.g. the Essenes) and some hoped for its destruction and a miraculous restoration of Solomon's Temple, 'not made by human hands'. Jesus is depicted as being against the Temple in various ways. In Mark 11:17 he causes a disturbance in the outer court by overturning the tables of the money changers. He claims a Scripture verse as his inspiration: 'My house shall be called a house of prayer for all the nations' (Isaiah 56:7). This act of disruption was a protest against the commercialisation of the Temple, as no Gentile money was allowed within the inner precincts. Money-changers offered Hebrew coinage at inflated exchange rates. Another tradition suggests that Jesus hoped for the destruction of Herod's Temple, and the establishment of a new order. John 2:19 has him saying: 'Destroy this temple and in three days I will raise it up'.

By the time of Jesus, Judaism had become less Temple-orientated. The synagogue had spread all over the Hellenistic world. These were often rooms in houses that were given over for religious meetings, where the Scriptures were read and discussed. These provided an alternative focus for many Jews in the Diaspora, scattered abroad. The synagogue had also taken root in the Holy Land itself. The study of the Scriptures had encouraged people to read and write. (In Jesus' day, the canon of the Jewish Bible – to become the Christian Old Testament – was not formally fixed, but was more or less so by popular consent. Ecclesiastes and Song of Songs were not included until late in the first century, though, and the apocryphal books were only included in the **Septuagint (LXX)** Greek Translation.) Texts found in the Dead Sea Scrolls suggest that there were many versions of the Old Testament texts, which were only normalised by the end of the first century AD.

The Temple was a centre of sacrifice, not of learning and discussion. Pious Jews travelled there on special occasions, such as the annual Passover celebration, to make their offerings and to share in meals. A.N. Wilson has described the Temple thus:

> … the Temple, for all its marble and gold, was really a magnificently constructed abattoir designed to ease, and ritualise relations between humanity and the Unseen.
>
> *Paul – the Mind of the Apostle*, p. 44

2 Religious parties

a) The Pharisees

This was a lay movement that had partly developed from the Hasidim in the Maccabean period, and began to emerge as a distinct group during the reign of the High Priest, John Hyrcanus (son of Simon Maccabaeus), at the close of the second century BC. They were a creative, progressive group, full of zeal and piety. Their name derives either from a Hebrew word meaning 'the separated' (as they were separated from the Temple priesthood, and from uncleanness) or it was a corruption of 'the Persians' in Hebrew, because they followed many of the new ideas that had been introduced into Judaism since the Persian period, when the Jews were under Persian control.

Their new beliefs included:

- The resurrection of the dead
- Angels and demons
- Providence – that God has a plan for history
- **Predestination** – that events in the future are foreordained and can therefore be predicted
- The **Halakoth**, the oral tradition about the Torah, has to be followed.

These new ideas included a strong belief in the after-life as a resurrection from the dead. Some also taught that there was an intermediate state where the righteous soul languished until the final resurrection, which was 'paradise' (a term derived from the Persian rulers' gardens). They also believed in angels and demons, beings which were only vaguely mentioned in the Old Testament Scriptures before the Persian period. They believed there was a divine plan at work in history, that would be fulfilled. Thus certain things could be predicted and promised by the prophets. This idea is called predestination.

The Pharisees are often accused of being legalistic. They followed the Torah, the Law of Moses, and they had the Halakoth, an oral tradition of how to follow the Torah in the different circumstances of their own day. They wanted to cover every circumstance of life with the Law of God as they saw it. Their motive was a practical holiness and a renewal of the religious life of the people. There were rival schools of interpretation: those of Rabbis Hillel and Shammai. Hillel was the more liberal in his interpretation of some verses of Scripture and laws, seeking to adapt these to his own day.

(i) Jesus and the Pharisees

The Pharisees have a bad name because of the Gospels. Jesus criticises them for hypocrisy; and harsh statements about their behaviour can be found in Matthew 23. Jesus' denunciation of them just does not fit historical fact; they were far from being the insincere legalists he makes them out to be. Naturally, some individuals among them might have been, and the words of Jesus might be based upon a genuine 'Jesus tradition' of speaking out against hypocrisy in religion (see Matthew 6:1–6 where the hypocrites are not named). Matthew probably adapted these words and made them his own stinging attack upon the Pharisees in a later time, when they had decided to prevent Jewish Christians from taking a part in the religious life of the people. The Pharisees were the dominant party after the fall of Jerusalem and the Temple in AD 70, when Judaism survived in the synagogues. Rabbi Johanan ben Zakkai set up the Academy at Jamnia, with his fellow rabbis, to replace the Sanhedrin. The Council held here, in AD 84, declared that various groups, including the Christians, were heretics. Earlier, in Acts, the Pharisees are portrayed as being sympathetic to the Christians (see Gamaliel's speech in Acts 5:33–40).

b) The Sadducees

The origin of the Sadducees is more obscure than that of the Pharisees. Their name may be derived from that of the High Priest Zadok, in David's time, but as they were supporters of the non-Zadokite Hasmoneans, a more likely derivation is from the Hebrew word *saddiq*: 'righteous'. They would have regarded themselves as the 'righteous ones', as traditional believers who rejected the new ideas held by the Pharisees; and they accepted only the books of the Torah as Scripture. They were of the priestly and aristocratic families who controlled the bureaucracy. They were conservative in beliefs and in politics. Their religious hope was for a blessed life on earth for those who followed the Torah faithfully. They rejected the ideas of divine intervention in history, and of predestination, so dear to the Pharisees. They were a pragmatic group, trying to negotiate the best deal for Judaea. They feared the ambitions and the wrath of Rome on the one hand, and the dangerous idealism of various Jewish groups on the other. They wanted to maintain the status quo for the sake of peace, however uneasy. They controlled the Temple administration and were left without any influence in the religious life of the people once it was destroyed in AD 70. Manson said of them, 'For ideals and programmes, we must look elsewhere'.

c) The Essenes

Josephus regarded the Essenes as the third party or 'philosophy' amongst the Jews. (Flavius Josephus *c.* AD 37– *c.* 100 was a Jewish historian, brought up in Palestine, who became a Roman citizen and lived in Rome for the last part of his life. He wrote about the Jewish people to convince his Roman contemporaries that they were a civilised race.) The Essenes are also mentioned by Philo, the Elder

Pliny and Hippolytus. Their works were written in Greek, and we have no Hebrew sources that describe the Essenes. This has led to much speculation about the meaning of 'Essene', and two Aramaic terms have been suggested. *Hasya* means 'holy, or pious ones', and could show that the Essenes were connected with the earlier Hasidim. *Asya* means 'healers' and would fit Philo's description of a Jewish group in Egypt called *therapeutoi*: 'the healers'.

Accounts of the Essenes suggest that they were a monastic group that practised celibacy, with their own baptismal rites of frequent washings for purification. They rejected the Temple priesthood, replacing the animal sacrifices with their own community meal. Josephus tells us that people were only admitted to this meal after three years spent as a novice. They pooled their money, and lived a communal lifestyle, meeting together on the Sabbath to study the Scriptures. Some were lay members, living in the cities with their families, and visiting for worship and study. Josephus says that there was a married order, raising children, and the wives joined in with the ritual washings. Pliny says that there was a group of Essenes at the Dead Sea; and the only settlement that archaeologists have found is at Qumran. The ruins show that there were baptismal pools, and the Scrolls reveal a distinctive method of scriptural study and commentary.

The Essenes were not pacifists; the Essene John was a leader during the war with Rome. The Scrolls reveal their plans for the final battle, when God would restore the Kingdom to Israel.

d) The Zealots

The **Zealots** called themselves *qannaim*, or *qananayya* (Hebrew and Aramaic: 'to be filled with zeal'). Their heroes were Phinehas, grandson of Aaron, who terminated a mixed marriage out of *zeal* for the Lord (recorded in Numbers 25:1–13), and the prophet Elijah who said, 'I have been very *zealous* for the Lord, the God of hosts' (1 Kings 19:10). In more recent times, they followed the example of Mattathias, father of Judas Maccabaeus. He 'burned with *zeal*' and killed a Jew who was about to offer sacrifice on a pagan altar.

Josephus, and the rabbinical writings, mention the Zealots as a party only during the Jewish War. Josephus mentions Judas the Galilean as the founder of the fourth party, however, leading a revolt in AD 6, and says that he taught that it was not lawful to acknowledge the sovereignty of a Gentile ruler. (This thought lies behind the question put to Jesus in Mark 12:14–17 about paying taxes to Caesar.) No doubt activists known as the Zealots in AD 66–70 were part of a long-standing resistance movement that went back to the Maccabees. Indeed, members of the other Jewish parties could be called Zealots too, if they took part in armed resistance in the name of Israel's God and of his Law. (Remember, also, the involvement of the Essenes in the Jewish revolt.) Another group mentioned by Josephus was the 'sikarioi' (Latin: *sicarii*), or 'the Assassins'. They took part in occasional revolts, and assassinated people in crowds during festivals. They should be linked with the general network of resistance that was led by the Zealots during the war with Rome.

Summary List

- **Jesus** taught between the victory of the Maccabees in the second century BC, and the fall of Jerusalem in AD 70.
- **The Jews** were ruled by client kings, installed by the Romans, until the death of Herod in 4 BC. Then the four tetrarchies were set up. Judaea was ruled directly by a prefect from AD 6.
- **Herod's Temple** was a grand building project which was the focus of sacrifice and worship for Judaism. There were schismatic groups and dissenters, though. They resented:
  - Herod's pagan attitudes;
  - the opulence of the Temple when it should have been a simpler place of worship;
  - the line of High Priests going back to 152 BC which replaced the Zadokite lineage going back to King David's time.
- **The Pharisees** were a popular lay movement, trying to teach the Torah locally, and applying oral traditions to cover every aspect of daily life. They had developed new ideas, such as resurrection and the role of angels.
- **The Sadducees** were the established ruling set and the landed gentry. Their policy towards Rome was one of appeasement. They rejected anything other than the Torah as Scripture.
- **The Essenes** were a separatist group with their own rituals and leaders, rejecting the Temple hierarchy.
- **The Zealots** were not a separate party but comprised anyone who believed in fighting for the freedom of the Jewish homeland.
- **Judaism** in the first century can be approached by the study of three themes: the Book, the Land and the Covenant.
  - *The Book*: the Torah/Cetubim/Nebiim (law/writings/Prophets). Authority, formation of canon, written and oral Law. Present disputes between Reform Jews and the Orthodox.
  - *The Land*: the significance of the land, the settlement in Canaan, the Deuteronomic history and glory/disgrace; the Exile and Restoration. Leviticus 25 and the Jubilee (the Land as Yahweh's with cancellation of all debts).
  - *The Covenant*: meaning; covenant of Abraham, Moses; and promises of new covenant in Jeremiah 31:33

Answering structured and essay questions on Chapter 4

1. Briefly list the main points you can find out about the following: **a)** Sadducees; **b)** Essenes; **c)** Zealots.

2. Read Acts 5:12-42 and Acts 23:1-10. How did the differences between the Sadducees and the Pharisees help the early Church?
3. 'Destroy this temple and in three days I will raise it up.' (John 2:19) Explain why some Jews would have shared Jesus' antipathy towards Herod's Temple.

5 The Covenant

KEYWORDS

covenant – special, binding agreement (*berith* in Hebrew, from a word meaning 'fetter')

Ba'al – 'lord', a Canaanite fertility god

Decalogue – the Ten Commandments

Deuteronomist – one editor of Torah traditions

Torah – the Law of Moses, the first five books of the Bible

Hesed – loving mercy

The biblical **covenants** derived from the Ancient Near Eastern forms of binding agreements, which might be between equals, or between a superior and an inferior, with obligations on one party or on both; e.g. the agreement between Gilgamesh, the king of Sumer, and Enkidu his faithful associate. Another example is of that between a victorious ruler and a conquered state, as in the Hittite treaties (*c.* 1400–1200 BC). These had lists of obligations, curses and blessings that affected the inferior party.

1 In the Old Testament

KEY ISSUE Various covenants are found in the OT:

- Noah's covenant – with all humanity
- Abraham's covenant – with his descendants
- Moses' covenant – with the Hebrews after the Exodus
- David's covenant – with the descendants of David

The Old Testament uses the word *berith*: 'covenant', or solemn agreement. It is probably from the same root as the Hebrew word for 'fetter', hence it was something binding. The word 'testament' is another English translation, suggesting a formal, binding agreement. The Greeks used the word *diatheke.*

a) The covenant with Noah (Genesis 9:8:17)

Here, the sign of the covenant is the rainbow, promising that the world will never again be destroyed by flood. This covenant is with all humanity, through Noah and his family, and with the creatures of the earth. God is bound by this covenant, with no conditions laid upon humanity.

b) The covenant with Abraham (Genesis 15:1–17:21)

Again, this covenant binds God to bless and preserve the descendants of Abraham, with the expectation that they will walk in faith (Genesis 15:6) and seek to be perfect before God (Genesis 17:1). The covenant with Abraham is concerned with descendants and with possession of land, things of paramount concern to wandering clans in the second millennium BC.

The historicity of the Genesis passages is debatable, and it is thought that various strands of tradition have been edited together as the people of Israel developed their history and their theology. The sign of circumcision, for example (Genesis 17), is assigned to the priestly source (P) dating from around the sixth–fifth centuries BC, which was concerned with outward signs and observances at a time when the Jews were in exile in Babylon. The people had to preserve their national and religious identity at all costs. (But was circumcision ever given such an interpretation by Abraham himself? It was a folk custom for many ancient people). The Abraham sagas probably contain historical truth; it was the custom for a clan leader to form a covenant with a deity for the clan's protection. A clan would worship and sacrifice to a god and seek its favours. The Abraham sagas show a primitive concern with early Canaanite shrines such as Mamre, and deities such as El Shaddai and El Elyon ('God Most High') e.g. Genesis 13:18; 14:18–20. ('El' was the general Semitic term for God or a god.)

c) The covenant with Moses and the people at Sinai (Exodus 24)

The covenant with the Hebrews after the Exodus from Egypt was one of a superior to an inferior, a ruler to a vassal, God to the people. This had obligations (the various laws and commandments) and was purely conditional, as the story of the golden calf shows (Exodus 32). Here, the covenant is broken before the people have even left the mountain, and Moses has to plead for mercy for them as God threatens to abandon them and make a covenant with the descendants of Moses alone. This conditional covenant is used by the D source, the **Deuteronomist** (*c.* 7th century BC), to write Israel's history theologically. In the story found in the books of Samuel and Kings, the blessing and peace under faithful kings, and the suffering and pestilence under unfaithful rulers, are seen as the results of obeying or rebelling against the covenant stipulations.

The giving of the **Decalogue**, the Ten Commandments, in Exodus 20:1–20 is cast in the form of the political treaties of the day, with a historical preamble showing why the people owed their allegiance to their lord (expressed in Exodus 20:2: God had rescued the people from slavery) and then has a list of stipulations (Exodus 20:3–20). Other parts of the OT have the other feature of the treaties, the lists of curses and blessings, such as Deuteronomy 27:14–28:6.

d) The covenant with David (2 Samuel 7:1–17, Psalm 2)

This covenant is binding on God alone, with the promise that God will bless the descendants of David and establish his throne forever. The language of sonship and divine fatherhood is introduced here (2 Samuel 7:14, Psalm 2:7) and this tradition forms the basis of the Messianic hope, that one anointed king from David's line will rule the people in peace and justice.

2 Images of the covenant

a) Commitment

Metaphors of deep human relationships – parent/child relationships, and of marital commitment and bonding – are used to picture God binding himself to his people in the covenant. So, God is a father or a mother to Israel (as in Isaiah 49:14–15, Jeremiah 3:19, Hosea 11:1–11); or like a husband to his wife (Isaiah 54:5–8, Hosea 2:16–20). The term *hesed* is used for God's affections for Israel: sometimes translated 'steadfast love' or 'covenant love'. The prophets agonise over the sins of the people, showing the mercy of God who feels the agony of betrayal (such as the 'adultery' of Israel in lusting after the Ba'als, the fertility gods of the Canaanites, as recorded in *Hosea*). This *hesed* of God is reflected in the traditions of the covenants with Abraham and David, everlasting covenants that are not conditional. Note that Moses pleads for the people at Sinai on the basis of Abraham's covenant (Exodus 32:13).

b) Responsibility

The sealing of the covenant and the passionate commitment to it by God suggest that the stipulations of the Law were based on gratitude for deliverance, and loving fidelity, and were not mere commandments and an imposition on the people; the people freely chose to belong to the Sinai covenant. The whole legal tradition of Israel, and the status of the Law, derived from the Sinai/Horeb traditions and the covenant with Moses, though many of the laws attached to these narratives are probably later additions. The Hebrew term for the Law

(**Torah**) is far richer than 'law', for it also suggests 'the way to follow', a gift and a guidance for people to use in life. This is the sense of the Law, as something to be loved, in Psalm 119:40–41:

> Behold, I long for thy precepts; in thy righteousness give me life! Let thy steadfast love come to me, O LORD...'.

c) A concern for justice

A regular theme in the OT prophets is the concern of God for the poor, the widow and the orphan. The Torah and the covenant demand righteousness. The prophet Amos denounced the complacent attitude of those who felt that God would protect them because of the covenant, even though they were oppressing the poor. He declared that the Lord despised their religious festivals and sacrifices because there was no justice in the land (Amos 5:21–24). These themes recur in the apocalyptic writings, with their vivid clashes of opposites: light and dark, angels and demons, life and death, present age and the age to come; the new world will be a restored paradise with justice and peace. Those in high places will be brought low, and the lowly will be exalted (cf also the preaching of John the Baptist in Luke 3:4–6, taken from Isaiah 40:3–5, and the Magnificat, Mary's song, Luke 1:51–53).

3 In the New Testament

KEY ISSUE Ezekiel and Jeremiah had prophesied the making of a new covenant after the breaking of the old Sinai covenant, as the people were sent into exile in Babylon, and the Temple of Solomon was destroyed *c.* 587 BC (Ezekial 36:23–28, Jeremiah 31:31–34). The blessings experienced through Christ were seen as the fulfilment of this. The New Testament idea is based upon the whole cluster of covenant traditions in the Old Testament.

a) Noah's covenant

The death of Christ effected a redemption for the whole of humanity and for the whole creation (see 2 Corinthians 5:19, Romans 8:18–23).

b) Abraham's covenant

This is richly woven into New Testament theology. Paul contrasts this covenant with that at Sinai, as a covenant of promise against one of condition and law. Abraham's covenant is one where people are justified by faith and not by their works; Gentiles can also be included because they can walk by faith (Romans 4). Paul contrasts Spirit and Law, and sees the new covenant as far superior to the old (Galatians 4:21–28; 2 Corinthians 3:12–18). This led him to set aside many of the legalistic demands of the Torah and to follow a Gospel of grace. Abraham freed Paul from Moses.

Paul's view of his life as a Pharisee was one of legalistic religion, a nagging, anxious zeal to be perfect, while being constantly aware of his failure and sinfulness (Romans 7). He seems to have had an anxious personality that could not believe his failings could be forgiven. Clearly, he had experienced a liberation through Christ, and an overwhelming sense of forgiveness and relief (compare Romans 8 with Romans 7). This view of the Torah as a set of guiding ideals that were a burden, impossible to live up to and always causing guilt, was not shared by many of his contemporaries, or the Jews of the Old Testament (compare the attitude to the Torah in Psalm 119). Hebrews shows an awareness of the eternal nature of the new covenant in Christ, and links this with the covenant with Abraham, and his blessing by Melchizedek, the ancient king of Salem (Hebrews 6:13–7:25). It is the Sinai covenant, with the Torah, that is temporary, and a shadow of that greater blessing and covenant that had come in Christ (Hebrews 10:1).

c) Moses' covenant

The rituals sealing this covenant are echoed in some of the Last Supper narratives (see Luke 22:20; 1 Corinthians 11:25, 'This cup is the new covenant in my blood...') where a sacred meal is held, and blood is then shed on the cross.

d) David's covenant

This is reflected in the language of divine sonship and fatherhood (as in Matthew 11:25–27) and the title 'Son of David' used of Jesus (Matthew 15:22).

e) Attitudes to the Torah

It should also be noted that the Pauline notion of the Torah being set aside by Christ, as a burden that no longer needed to be borne, is not followed through consistently in the New Testament. There is the enigmatic saying about the abiding nature of the Torah in Matthew 5:17–19 and the evidence of controversy over Judaising amongst Gentile converts, such as is found in Galatians and in the Council of Jerusalem in Acts 15. In Acts 21:17–26 Paul purifies himself according to Jewish custom. The attitude to the Torah in James is very different from that in Paul's epistles.

The solemn pledge of God to his creation, with Noah, with Abraham, with Moses and with David, is seen as finding its most sublime fulfilment in the flesh of Christ, as love goes through the cross to redeem the world. The Mass, Eucharist, or Holy Communion is a ritual celebration of the death of Christ. This is seen as a sacrifice for sin, and the blood that sealed the new covenant

Summary List

- A covenant is a binding agreement which obligates two parties in some way.
- Covenants between God and his people occur several times in the OT: Noah/ Abraham/ Moses/ David.
- Covenant themes are of commitment, responsibility and justice. *Hesed* is a key covenant term, meaning 'steadfast love'.
- The NT claims to be the new covenant promised in the prophets after the failure of the people of Israel and their Exile to Babylon. God's blessings are channelled through Christ to the whole world. Whereas Moses' covenant was central to Judaism, Paul makes this limited and temporary by appealing to the earlier promises given to Abraham. He sees Christ as the fulfilment of these.

Answering structured and essay questions on Chapter 5

1. For the covenants made with Noah, Abraham, Moses and David, list what details you can find out to show **a)** on whose behalf it was made, **b)** who was bound by it, and **c)** what obligations were attached to it.
2. Look up the following references and list the metaphors for God's caring relationship with his people: Hosea 11:1–4; Isaiah 49:14–15; Hosea 2:16–23; Ephesians 5:22–27; Romans 8:15–16; Revelation 19:6–9.
3. How does the NT use some of the OT concepts of the covenant in its idea of Christ bringing the new covenant?

6 Use of the Old Testament

KEYWORDS

allegory – finding a hidden, symbolic meaning in a text

midrash – the exposition of a text, following various rules and looking for any hidden meanings and links with other passages

pesher – interpretation of a particular text

Talmud – collection of Rabbinical teachings written down after the first century AD

targum – translation of Hebrew texts of the OT into Aramaic. Some interpretative details were added

typology – seeing a type or reference to a future event in an earlier one, so Moses bringing water from the rock is a type of Christ bringing the Spirit

1 Introduction

The Old Testament can be discerned as an influence throughout the New Testament documents. It is obviously so in works such as Matthew and John, with the phrase 'in order that it might be fulfilled' in Romans 9–11, the early speeches in Acts, and Hebrews. The Old Testament exerted a more hidden influence on the rest of the New Testament: C H Dodd called it the 'substructure of New Testament theology', and Dunn feels that two unifying themes were present in early Christianity: Jesus and the Old Testament, though the Old Testament was read in the light of the life of Christ.

The content of the Old Testament was not static in the first century AD: the Law and the Prophets were, but the Writings were varied, and not all Jews accepted them as Scripture. The Septuagint (LXX) contained some works that the final form of the Hebrew text, the Masoretic text, ignored. The Epistle of Jude in the New Testament quotes from *1 Enoch*, a work which was not finally accepted as Scripture.

2 Jewish use of the Hebrew Scriptures

KEY ISSUE The Jews had five methods of interpreting their Bible (the Christian Old Testament): *targum, midrash, pesher,* typology and allegory.

a) *Targum*

Targum means 'translation', and the *targumim* (pl.) were translations of biblical books into Aramaic, the main language spoken by the Jews from the fifth century BC until the first century AD. They were very free translations, paraphrases, including interpretations of the text. For example, rather than use the bold phrase, 'they heard the sound of the Lord God walking in the cool of the Garden' (Genesis 3:8) the writers would write, 'they heard the sound of the word of the Lord God walking...' The *targum* of Isaiah 53 was careful to add details to avoid any Christian interpretation: the healing the Servant brought was to be the rebuilding of the Temple, after it had been destroyed.

b) *Midrash*

Midrash means 'exposition' of a text or passage. The interpreter would look for hidden meanings and any contemporary relevance. Hillel had seven rules of interpretation, such as finding a linking word or concept between different passages and then grouping them together. Later, 32 rules were developed. Two broad styles of midrash existed: Halakah and Haggadah. Halakah was concerned with specific rules of conduct read out of passages or events in the Sciptures. Haggadah was a much freer, imaginative telling of a story, with details added to draw out the meaning.

In the New Testament, John 6:31–58 can be seen as a *midrash* on Psalm 78:24, 'he gave them bread from heaven to eat.' 2 Corinthians 3:7–18 is a *midrash* on Exodus 34:29–35, the glory of the Lord shining in the face of Moses. M Goulder feels that the Gospel writers felt free to *midrash* other Gospels, so that Matthew's parable of the ten virgins (Matthew 25:1–12) is a *midrash* on Mark's command, 'Watch, therefore, for you do not know when the master of the house will come...' (Mark 13:35–37)

c) *Pesher*

Pesher is a narrower form of *midrash,* meaning 'interpretation'. (It is used frequently in Daniel 2:4–7:28 when dreams are interpreted.) At Qumran, a prophecy would be repeated, and then its *pesher* given, so that Habakkuk 1:6, which spoke of the Chaldeans, was seen as a reference to the Romans. In the New Testament, Matthew 27:9–10 is a *pesher* of Zechariah 11:13, drawing upon the theme of the thirty pieces of silver. Psalm 68:18 is subjected to a *pesher* in Ephesians 4:8, where the actual text is changed when it is quoted, to carry a new meaning.

d) Typology

Typology tries to find a one-to-one correspondence or analogy between events of the past and present or future events. So, David's reign was a type of the eschatological reign of God in the Old Testament, of Isaiah 11:1; and Eden was a type of the Messianic Age, Isaiah 11:6–8. In the New Testament, the events of the Exodus become types for the work of Christ and for baptism, as in 1 Corinthians 10:6; and in 1 Peter 3:21 Noah's ark on the waters becomes a type of baptism.

e) Allegory

Here the text is seen as a code with a simple literal meaning, and a hidden deeper meaning. Philo used the Old Testament like this widely, finding philosophical truths hidden under the various rituals, laws and stories. Paul used **allegory** in Galatians 4:22–31 where the children of Abraham, Ishmael and Isaac signify different relationships to God through the old covenant and the new.

3 Early Christian use of the Old Testament

KEY ISSUE Matthew uses the following Old Testament passages to support his Birth Narrative:

- Isaiah 7:14 for the virgin birth
- Micah 5:2 for the Messiah's birth in Bethlehem
- Hosea 11:1 for the flight of the Holy Family to Egypt
- Numbers 24:17 for the star of Bethlehem
- Isaiah 60:3 for the visit of the kings
- Isaiah 11:1 for the name 'Nazarene'

The birth story in Matthew (1:18–2:23) is an excellent example of Jewish-Christian use of the Old Testament viewed in the light of Christ. Four OT passages are quoted, with the fulfilment formula; and a number of indirect OT allusions can also be discerned. The whole sequence seems to be built around the OT passages like building blocks.

a) Explicit references to the Old Testament

- *Matthew 1:23* is the LXX version of Isaiah: 7:14. The Hebrew version is more ambiguous, for it could mean 'virgin' or 'young woman'. Even the Greek could carry the meaning of 'young woman' rather than someone who was literally a virgin. The original context was that a woman would give birth to a ruler of the Jews who would rescue them from the political troubles of the time, and would bless the people with peace. It was likely that the prophet thought this would happen in his own day. Matthew has taken this and applied it to the birth of Christ, years later, and sees a reference to Mary's virginity in it. The passage is used because it has a correspondence with the birth of Christ.
- *Matthew 2:6*. The Messiah is to be born in Bethlehem, according to Micah 5:2. It is interesting that Matthew does not say that Mary and Joseph travelled there for the birth; Luke tells that story. Otherwise, they seem to be resident at Nazareth.
- *Matthew 2:15*. The claim that Hosea 11:1 is fulfilled in the flight to and from Egypt does violence to the original context. Hosea referred to the Exodus from Egypt, where the whole of Israel was designated 'my son'. Matthew feels able to apply this general statement about Israel to Jesus, the Messiah.
- *Matthew 2:18*. Jeremiah 31:15 referred to the Exile of the Jews to Babylon and the despair of the people for their homeland. Matthew sees a correspondence with the weeping mothers who lose their children and claims that this verse is fulfilled in the event. This fulfilment seems more imaginative than actual, for its original context meant something quite different. Matthew feels at liberty to reread the whole of the Old Testament in the light of Christ.

b) Implicit references to the Old Testament

- *Matthew 2:1–2*. The wise men story might refer to Numbers 24:17 'a star shall come forth out of Jacob'; Psalm 72:10 'may the kings of Sheba and Seba bring gifts'; or Isaiah 60:3 'and nations shall come to the brightness of your light, and kings to the brightness of your rising.'
- *Matthew 2:23*. The appeal to the prophets that the Messiah will be called a Nazarene is not actually written anywhere in the Old Testament. It might refer to Isaiah 11:1 'A shoot shall rise from Jesse, and a branch [*neser*] shall sprout from his roots' The name of the town, Nazareth, sounds like the word for branch, one of the Messianic titles. Again, we see a very creative use of the Old Testament and not a literal reading.

A final question is whether the author of Matthew invented his birth story around these Old Testament verses, making them fit into the Jesus story (as some scholars maintain) or whether he searched through the Sciptures, noting anything that corresponded with the story he had received in the Jesus tradition.

c) Rabbis and Jesus

A search through the writings of the Rabbis from the period, such as the *Palestinian* ***Talmud***, reveals a common thought world with Jesus. There are some sayings, passages and parables that are strikingly similar to material found in the Gospels, such as this extract from Berakhot 2:8, from the *Palestinian Talmud*:

> With whom is Rabbi Bun son of Hiyya to be compared? With a king who hired several labourers. Among them was one labourer who was particularly zealous. What did the king do? He took this labourer for walks, long and short. In the evening the labourers came to receive their pay, and the king gave this labourer the full day's pay just as he gave the others. At that the labourers grumbled and said, 'We have worked hard the whole day and he worked only two hours and still received the same pay as we did.' To that the king rejoined: 'This labourer has achieved more in two hours than you with your hard work throughout the whole day' So Rabbi Bun has achieved more in twenty-eight years in respect to the study of the Torah than another proven scholar could have learned in a hundred years.'

Compare this with the parable of the labourers in the vineyard in Matthew 20:1–16.

Summary List

The OT was the only Bible used by the early Church. It has been called the 'substructure of NT theology.'

The NT harnessed all the following methods of dealing with the OT:

- ***Targum*** was a free translation from Hebrew into Aramaic, adding commentary to the text
- ***Midrash*** was a method of exposition, with a stricter or more imaginative style that found all kinds of links with words and ideas
- ***Pesher*** was a method of interpreting particular words or verses
- **Typology** sought a symbolic identity between events in the OT narrative e.g. Eden was a type of the Kingdom of God
- **Allegory** saw a hidden, symbolic meaning in OT stories.

Answering structured and essay questions on Chapter 6

1. Compare these two passages, and note how the New Testament one has been interpreted and adapted. What techniques have been used to do this (e.g. *midrash*, *pesher*)?

> Thou didst ascend the high mount,
> leading captives in thy train,
> and receiving gifts among men,
> even among the rebellious, that the
> LORD God may dwell there.

Psalm 68:18

(This Psalm probably referred to the Israelite king taking his throne, while God reigned from the Temple in Jerusalem; the reign of the king being a symbol of God's reign. Though this verse says that the king received gifts, later translations by the rabbis suggested that it was Moses being referred to here, who *gave* the gift of the Torah to the people. The New Testament writer of Ephesians probably knew of this version.)

> But grace was given to each of us according to the measure of Christ's gift. Therefore it is said,
> 'When he ascended on high he led a host of captives, and he gave gifts to men.'
> (In saying, 'He ascended,' what does it mean but that he had also descended into the lower parts of the earth? He who descended is also he who ascended far above all the heavens, that he might fill all things.) And his gifts were that some should be apostles, some prophets, some evangelists, some pastors and teachers …
>
> *Ephesians 4:7–11*

(The writer makes the Old Testament passage refer to the death, burial and resurrection of Christ; the gifts are the ministries in the Church.)

2. **a)** Read the Passion story in Matthew 27:32–66 and note any connections with Psalm 22:1,7–8,18 and Psalm 69:21.
b) Read the account of Judas' payment in Matthew 27:3–10. How does this compare with Zechariah 11:12–13 and Jeremiah 32:6–15; 18:2–3? How might *pesher* have been used here?

3. How does Paul use allegory in Galatians 4:21-31?

4. How does Matthew's birth story use OT methods of exegesis?

7 What is Apocalyptic?

KEYWORDS

apocalyptic – vivid poetry and symbolism that describes the rebirth of the world

eschatology – end time events

Exile – the Jews were exiled to Babylon in the sixth century BC

pseudopigraphy – 'false authorship' – ascribing your work to another author whom you admire

Wisdom – a tradition of wise advice and inner enlightenment

Zadokite – the high priestly line going back to Zadok at the time of King David

1 Introduction

KEY ISSUE **Apocalyptic** is a genre of religious literature that uses vivid imagery and bizarre symbols to present ideas about the purposes of God in the history of the world. It often deals with the end time (**eschatology**), claiming to reveal the future.

Events are set against the background of a cosmic struggle between good and evil, and contrasted with a final vision of a new world. The supernatural realm is described in the form of visions of angels, demons and the after-life. The term 'apocalyptic' is Greek for revelation, or unveiling. The hidden knowledge is handed on in the form of symbols, such as a battle between beasts and a man (Daniel 7:7–14); dates and seasons are suggested in the numbers of days or weeks (Daniel 7:25b; 8:14).

Another feature of apocalyptic is the anonymity of the authors. They claimed the names of great heroes or prophets of the Old Testament, such as Daniel, Moses, Isaiah or Enoch, to achieve a wide readership for their works, and to suggest that their teachings were a true interpretation of the purposes of God revealed in the Scriptures. This literary device is known as **pseudopigraphy** ('false authorship') and was accepted as a literary technique and not as dishonesty.

2 The origins of apocalyptic

The exact origin of this literary genre is debated. It is widely thought that it began with the return of the Jews from **Exile** in Babylon in the fifth century BC. Their release by King Cyrus of the Persians created fervent hopes of their becoming a great nation again, as they had been under David and Solomon. They longed for a return to their Golden Age. They had a High Priest, Joshua, who claimed to be in true lineage of the **Zadokite** priesthood instituted by David. There was no king, though, or heir in the line of David. According to Haggai, the governor of Judah, Zerubbabel, was seen in this light by the people. Haggai hails him as the chosen one (Haggai 2:23), a Messianic title, though Judah continued to be run as a theocracy under the High Priest during the Persian period. Haggai also uses apocalyptic imagery in 2:22. Here is a full-blooded eschatology with earth-shaking events. In the absence of a strong nation or king, Haggai appeals to God to restore the glory of the people.

Such hopes had been expressed in less catastrophic imagery in Isaiah (chapter 39 onwards) for example Isaiah 43:19–21; 44:23, and the hope of a 'Day of the Lord' was preached as early as the eighth century BC by prophets such as Amos. This seems to have been a time of judgement, and a restoration of the Kingdom. Apocalyptic went beyond this with cosmic imagery and a completely new world. Daniel uses apocalyptic in chapters 7–12, and is thought to date from the second century BC when the Jews were being persecuted by Antiochus Epiphanes in his attempt to make them follow Hellenistic customs and religious practices. The beasts represent various rulers and nations, which are overthrown by the saints of God after a period of suffering. An apocalyptic passage also appears in Isaiah 24–27 and this is thought to be either a later addition, or a very early example of the genre that might pre-date the Persian period.

(There are other apocalyptic works not included in the books of the Old Testament. There are several, such as *The Assumption of Moses*, *The Testament of Levi*, the *Book of Enoch* and various passages and themes found in the Dead Sea Scrolls.)

Others suggest an external influence for the rise of apocalyptic, namely that of Persian religion, Zoroastrianism, which had flourished since the sixth century BC. This taught that there would be a final victory of good over evil, and that there would be a cosmic conflict between light and darkness until the end came. The Jews in Exile in Babylon would have come into contact with this.

Some give internal reasons for the rise of apocalyptic: the reinterpretation of old texts and hopes for a 'Day of the Lord' after the return from Exile; or a development of the **Wisdom** thought of the OT which stressed esoteric and personal knowledge bypassing an organised priesthood (for example the Qumran community which rejected the Temple and its priesthood). Again, ancient myths and stories could have been rewritten, e.g. the battle between Ba'al the nature god, and Yamm, the force of chaos, represented as the seas or as a dragon in the Canaanite myths. (This conflict had been used of Yahweh, the Lord, e.g. in Psalm 74:12–14, and the crossing of the Sea of Reeds was seen as the victory of God over chaos, as was the creation of the world from the waters in Genesis 1:1–2.) This conflict was then the eschatological conflict. The myths of the Creation and preservation of the world against chaos become the power of God breaking into the world to make all things new, restore the Kingdom to Israel, and raise the dead.

In summary, various movements might have contributed to the rise of apocalyptic:

- National hopes
- Persian religion
- The Wisdom tradition
- The reworking of old, Canaanite myths.

3 Apocalyptic themes

a) Dualism

The writings present contrasts between light and darkness, the flesh and the spirit, angels and demons, the present age and the age to come. This is an ethical dualism, a conflict between good and evil with a final victory of good. (see Dead Sea Scrolls refer to the 'children of light' and the 'children of darkness'.)

b) Angels and demons

There is very little mention of either angels or demons in the Old Testament before the Persian period. There is the 'angel of the Lord' who leads the Hebrews out of Egypt, and there is a heavenly court, the *elohim*, who are probably the demoted Canaanite gods. There is sin and evil, but no personal Devil or devils. Satan appears in Job, thought to be a late work from the Persian period, and hierarchies of angels and demons appear in the apocalyptic writings (e.g. the archangels Michael, Gabriel and Raphael, and the various names for the prince of evil, Satan, Azazel, Beliar, Beelzebub) some of these names are not in the Canon of Scripture, but occur in inter-testemental writings. It is likely that Jewish angelology and demonology developed under Persian influence, with their belief in good and evil spirits.

c) Resurrection

The belief in the resurrection of the dead in a new world was a late development in Judaism, and is attested only in Isaiah 26:19 and Daniel 12:2–3 in the OT. This is an apocalyptic theme, and might have been partly influenced by Zoroastrian ideas of a final judgement, with individual rewards and punishments.

d) The coming deliverer

The idea of a Messiah as a king in the line of David had been in the Old Testament since the monarchy, but the idea emerged in the apocalyptic writings in a new way: he is often a more supernatural figure. If Daniel 7:13–14 ('one like a son of man') is a Messianic passage, then the idea of a supernatural liberator is attested here.

The idea of a supernatural Messiah is in the *Testament of Levi*:

> His star will arise in heaven like that of a king, and light the light of knowledge as the sun does the day. He will be magnified in the world, and shine forth on the earth like the sun, and remove all darkness under heaven. There will be peace in all the earth ...

Some apocalyptic writings suggest that God himself will intervene without a Messiah and change the world, e.g. the *Assumption of Moses*:

> For the Heavenly One will arise from His royal throne, and He will go forth from His holy dwelling, with indignation and wrath on account of his children. The earth will tremble and be shaken to its depths ...

4 Apocalyptic in the New Testament

The Apocalypse, or the Book of Revelation, is an apocalyptic work concerning the end time using bizarre imagery for the final conflict. Here Jesus is portrayed as the 'one like a son of man' in Daniel as he brings in the Kingdom, defeats the Devil, and brings in the new world. It is a poetic work, teaching one basic point, that good will win over evil, that Christ is the saviour of the world. When the author thought all this would take place is irrelevant; he probably wrote it in a time of persecution, hoping for an imminent *parousia* (return of Christ). Today we can draw religious inspiration from its theme of good winning over evil, and of there being a goal to history.

That Jesus was an apocalyptic teacher can be seen in various Gospel passages, (e.g. Mark 13; Matthew 24–25; Luke 21). Mark 13 underlies the other two Gospels, which expand the material. Mark might have used a separate source, a 'little apocalypse' that circulated among the early Christians. This uses earth-shaking imagery, and refers to Daniel 7:13:

> But in those days, after that tribulation, the sun will be darkened, and the moon will not give its light, and the stars will be falling from heaven, and the powers in the heavens will be shaken. And then they will see the Son of man coming in clouds with great power and glory.
>
> *Mark 13:24–26*

Apocalyptic imagery, and a sense of a coming crisis, is seen in Mark 8:38; 9:1, and in the parable of the net in Matthew 13:47–50.

However, a different type of eschatology can also be found in the Gospels: that of growth and discovery, as in the parables of the sower, the weeds in the field, the hidden treasure, and the pearl (Matthew 13:1–46). In Luke 17:21 the Kingdom is within the believer, or among them. Dodd reads Mark 1:15 'The Kingdom of God is at hand' as 'The Kingdom is here, now!' (i.e. in Jesus). This 'realised eschatology' is that the Kingdom can be found within the heart, and discovered in this life, and not just in the age to come.

Summary List

How did apocalyptic begin?

Eighth century	Early OT prophets, such as Amos, warned of a coming 'day of the Lord'.
Sixth century	Persian influence might have been involved, as the religion of Zoroastrianism taught a final struggle between good and evil.
Fifth century	When the Exiles returned from Babylon, they had no king. People looked to God as their King and Deliverer, and hoped for divine intervention to bring a new king.
Second century	A reaction to persecution. A stress on Wisdom and individual guidance undermined the regular cult of priests and the Temple. Old myths were rethought and rewritten, hoping for God's reign to dawn on earth.

Main points in apocalyptic

- There is a cosmic struggle between good and evil.
- There will be a new world.
- There are vivid visions of angels, demons and the after-life.
- Hidden meanings are revealed in numbers and old stories.

Answering structured and essay questions on Chapter 7

1. Describe the apocalyptic style of Jesus' teaching in Mark 13. How does this use ideas in Daniel 7:13?
2. Compare the parables of Jesus in Matthew 13. Say which use apocalyptic imagery and which do not.
3. 'The kingdom of God is in the midst of you' (Luke 17:21). How far do you consider this to summarise the teaching of Jesus on the Kingdom of God?

a) Planning an essay

Use the following plan to write an essay on question 3 above.

i) Introduction

The proclamation of the Kingdom is a major feature of the teaching of Jesus in the Synoptic Gospels e.g. Mark 1:15, as against the epistles, where Jesus and his return are preached. But is this an already present or future Kingdom? What does it mean to say the Kingdom of God is 'at hand'?

ii) A present reality

Luke 17:20–21 and the kingdom within.
Parables of growth, e.g. the sower (Matthew 13:3–9), the mustard seed (31–32) and the yeast (33). Here, the kingdom is consummated gradually, from within, without a final crisis.
Parables of discovery: e.g. the hidden treasure, the pearl of great price (Matthew 13:44–45). The Kingdom is in our midst, waiting to be discovered and lived out.
Matthew 11:2–6 and the miracles of Jesus as signs of the Kingdom present and active on earth. Jesus as the Kingdom in person.
All the above known as 'realised eschatology'. C H Dodd argued that this was part of the primitive Gospel tradition.

iii) A coming crisis

Matthew 24–25; Mark 13; Luke 21 and apocalyptic imagery. Note the coming of the Son of Man prediction.
Parables of crisis e.g. the parable of the fish net (Matthew 13:47–50). (The wheat and the tares (Matthew 13:24–29) is a mixed parable about growth and a final crisis.) Scholars such as Wrede and Albert Schweitzer argued that this crisis eschatology was the primitive Gospel tradition, and the early Church toned it down in favour of a realised eschatology, when the *parousia* was delayed and Jerusalem had fallen.

iv) Conclusion

There are two strands of tradition in the Gospels that can both claim to be the primitive tradition. The parable of the wheat and the tares suggests that the two could be combined, and they might have been preached as different aspects of the mystery of the coming of the Kingdom by Jesus and the early Church. Jeremias has argued that we must speak of an eschatology 'in the process of realization': there in the person of Jesus, in the hearts of believers through the gift of the Holy Spirit, but incomplete, and still awaiting a future consummation.

In the book *The Shadow of the Galilean* by Gerd Theissen, a Jewish merchant called Andreas is arrested by the Romans and interrogated. He lies in a dark cell, afraid, and he has a dream:

> Before me was Pilate in his purple-striped toga. He kept saying, 'I'm not inhuman, I'm not a beast.' His features turned into a caricature. Great teeth sprouted in his mouth. His hands were clenched. Where the ring gleamed on his finger I could see claws. His body swelled up until a giant animal, a spitting monster stood in front of me, which arrogantly threatened the whole world with its paws and kept hissing, 'I'm not inhuman, I'm not a beast.'
>
> I wanted to run away, but my legs wouldn't move. I couldn't budge. Instead, the monster got nearer, and now it was snapping at my feet. Its paws touched my knees, and then it reared up to seize me by the throat. But suddenly it winced, cringed and grew small; it whimpered and writhed in the dust. All its pride and glory had disappeared, as though it were prostrate before an invisible power standing behind me.
>
> I turned round. Behind me was a man. People surrounded him. They brought books. In them were written the crimes of the beast, not only the misdeeds of Pilate but those of the whole Roman empire. One crime after another was read out – and each time the beast whimpered and writhed in the dust. Finally the verdict was given: the beast was removed and killed. The man and his entourage took over its rule.
>
> *The Shadow of the Galilean*, p. 25

Later, Andreas has another, similar dream, after he has heard about Jesus of Nazareth, and he recognises the man in the dream as Jesus:

> It was Jesus, a changed Jesus. I had only seen him once – from the city wall of Jerusalem. At that time he was hanging dead on the cross, but now he radiated life, peace and freedom. The rule of the beasts was at an end. I woke up, happy, but confused.
>
> *The Shadow of the Galilean*, p. 184

The author has used apocalyptic imagery to express the deepest hopes and fears of Andreas, a first-century Jew. The beasts and the man are based upon Daniel 7, and the four beasts there are meant to be the Babylonians, Medes, Persians and Greeks. Later writers saw the fourth beast as Rome.

Think about how we might write apocalyptic today, to express our hopes and fears. For example, at one point in *The Shadow of the Galilean,* Andreas dreams of our modern world, where two giant octopuses are fed by workers who are given very little in return, until the two creatures start to wage a horrific war on each other, threatening to engulf the whole world. Who do you think the two octopuses represent, and who are the workers who feed them?

8 The Search for the Historical Jesus

KEYWORDS

Aramaisms – Aramaic terms used in the Gospels without translating them

Christ of faith – the interpretation of Jesus by the early Church after the Resurrection

canonical criticism – reading a passage in the context of the whole Bible aids understanding

Cynics – A Greek philosophical movement of wandering teachers who begged their food and spoke in short, witty sayings.

form criticism – tracing the form of individual units and arguing for their shape in the period of oral transmission

Gospel – the 'good news' that Jesus is the Christ, the Messiah

Jesus of history – the bare facts about the man Jesus

Kingdom of God – the rule of God on earth

literary criticism – studying the final form of the text as a literary work

Sitz im Leben – 'life setting', the situation that a unit of tradition originally addressed in the early Church

sociological criticism – tracing social themes in units of Gospel tradition

source criticism – tracing the sources used by the evangelists in each Gospel

Trajectory Theory – the idea that primitive material might be found in later, heretical Christian texts, and a common pattern, or trajectory could be found by comparing all of these sources with the Synoptics.

1 Introduction

KEY ISSUE Scholars have long debated the reliability of the Gospels as historical accounts of the life of Jesus. Who was Jesus? A wonder worker? A freedom fighter? A new prophet? A holy teacher? A philosopher? A preacher of the end of the world? God incarnate?

The earliest **Gospel** (Mark) was written at least thirty years after Jesus' death, and the fourth Gospel was probably written at the end of the first century. A hard question has to be asked: did the early Church invent a divine, exalted, risen Christ who had little in fact to do with the Galilean rabbi called Jesus of Nazareth? Christians claim that the man Jesus is the bringer of God's salvation and Kingdom, who reigns at the right hand of the Father in glory. These claims are striking and unique.

The first three Gospels present a very similar view of Jesus, at variance with that of John and, to some extent, with the Christ preached in the epistles, even those written before the Gospels. (Matthew, Mark and Luke are known as the Synoptic Gospels because they all tell a similar story, seen from the same point of view.) The Synoptic Christ is a preacher of the coming **Kingdom of God**; he has a charismatic effect on people, calls the outcasts of society to join his disciples, works miracles of healing, and is mysteriously raised from the dead. He does not claim to be God on earth, or even the Son of God in so many words. He is wary even of being called the Messiah. But in John this striking figure is clearly God on earth, who knows of his prior existence with the Father in glory. In the Epistles, he is the Lord who became man, and was then raised up and exalted (see, for example, Philippians 2:6–11). The proclaimer of the Kingdom becomes the one who is proclaimed by the first Christians; there is a significant shift in the message and the portrait of Jesus that is presented.

2 What is a Gospel?

It is accepted that the Gospels are not simply historical documents, but are intended to be proclamations about Jesus, to create faith in him (John 20:31). They are preaching-books, and not factual records of what Jesus said and did. When the Synoptics are compared, significant differences can be seen in the way certain events are reported or interpreted, such as Mark 6:45–52 compared with Matthew 14:22–33. Here, Matthew adds the theme of discipleship to the story of Peter walking on the water. That is his concern in telling the story, whereas for Mark it is a simple 'wonder tale' about Jesus. Bornkamm states that Matthew is 'an interpreter of the tradition he has collected and arranged'.

Each Gospel writer presents Jesus in his own way:

- *Matthew*: the fulfiller of Judaism, and as a new Moses giving a new Law;
- *Mark*: a charismatic wonder worker;
- *Luke*: the one in whom the Kingdom dawns for all nations;
- *John*: God made man.

Wrede even suggested that the outline story in the Synoptics (the start of the ministry at his baptism, the ministry in Galilee and then in Jerusalem for his final week) is Mark's construction, as he loosely collected together traditions about Jesus: parables, sayings, miracle stories and Passion narrative.

3 Lives of Jesus

The Gospels present Jesus in different ways. Various scholars in the eighteenth and nineteenth centuries tried to tease out the factual material from later Christian ideas and preaching. They were sceptical about the miraculous, and any claims that Jesus made about himself. They argued for a gentle Jesus who taught the brotherhood of humanity and the Fatherhood of God.

Albert Schweitzer, at the end of the nineteenth century, wrote a critique of all these lives of Jesus in his *The Quest of the Historical Jesus.* He felt that people were trying to find a Jesus that suited them, rather than one that challenged them. He believed there had to be a strangeness about Jesus to disturb modern believers and make them think.

> There was a danger that we should offer them a Jesus who was too small, because we had forced Him into conformity with our human standards and human psychology. Many of the greatest sayings are found lying in a corner like explosive shells from which the charges have been removed. No small portion of elemental religious power needed to be drawn off from His sayings to prevent them from conflicting with our system of religious world-acceptance. In the process we ourselves have been enfeebled ...
>
> *The Quest of the Historical Jesus*, p. 398

> Jesus means something to our world because a mighty spiritual force streams forth from Him and flows through our time also. This fact can neither be shaken nor confirmed by any historical discovery. It is the solid foundation of Christianity.
>
> *The Quest of the Historical Jesus*, p. 397

4 The Christ of faith

a) Bultmann

This New Testament scholar felt that there was very little interest about the life and teaching of the earthly Jesus in the early Church: they were only interested in the present Jesus, the risen Lord who guided his Church. He quotes Paul in 2 Corinthians 5:16: Christ was no longer known in the flesh, but by the Spirit.

Bultmann is sceptical about how much of the career of the historical Jesus could be traced in the Gospels, even in the Synoptics, for he feels that the original teaching of Jesus had been completely reinterpreted by the early Church in the light of their belief in the divinity and resurrection of Jesus. Even the miracle stories could have been products of faith : the first believers felt a new life within, and so they embellished the Jesus story with 'wonder tales'.

According to Bultmann, the words of Jesus in the Gospels were more likely to be those of the first Christians, putting their beliefs on his lips, e.g. the titles describing Jesus, or ethical teaching such as in Matthew 22:15–22. (Bultmann feels that some of the early communities had arguments about paying the Temple tax, and so this was written into the Gospels.) He sees the Gospels as a kind of folk-literature, being created by the daily experiences and imaginations of the first Christians.

Bultmann followed the liberal critics of the past century who had tried to write a historical life of Jesus in which they rejected the miraculous, feeling that this was not scientific. They had to alter many Gospel passages. Albert Schweitzer criticised them for projecting the ideas of the authors onto the person of Jesus; they made him in their image. He proceeded to do the same in *The Quest of the Historical Jesus* by claiming that Jesus was really an apocalyptic prophet. Bultmann reacted against the various portraits of Jesus by stressing the role of faith and the role of the exalted Lord in early Christianity, bypassing the problem in this way. Whoever Jesus had been, he was *now* the risen Lord.

b) Bornkamm

This theologian, in *Jesus of Nazareth*, was more positive than Bultmann. He felt that a commitment to the *historical* person of Jesus and his teaching had to precede any act of interpretation. The telling of his story was not static, though. It was a creative, dynamic process, that took the words of Jesus and recast them in a form for today, for the 'today' of Matthew's Church, or Mark's Church, or whatever. So, an original parable about a wedding feast can come to life in two different ways in the Jesus tradition, in Matthew 22:1–14 and Luke 14:16–24. Jesus continues to have an impact upon his followers :

> And yet we must never lose sight of the fact that, precisely in this way of transmitting and recounting, the person and work of Jesus, in their unmistakable uniqueness and distinctiveness, are shown forth with an originality which again and again far exceeds and disarms even all believing understandings and interpretations. Understood in this way, the primitive tradition of Jesus is brim full of history.
>
> *Jesus of Nazareth*, pp. 25–6

c) Robinson

J M Robinson in *A New Quest of the Historical Jesus* pointed out that different approaches were used in the twentieth century from those of the nineteenth. The latter were concerned with dates and facts, but the contemporary emphasis is upon interpretation, and the self-consciousness of the writer, or the impact of events upon him or her. Thus, the personality of Jesus stands behind all the work of the early Christians, inspiring their faith and commitment. Something made them respond to him in the way they did.

There is no longer any attempt to write lives of Jesus, except by fundamentalist Christians. More conservative scholars are content to point out probabilities, and to show how certain features of the Jesus tradition might well be genuinely historical.

A final comment must be that if some sayings of Jesus were put onto his lips after the resurrection, this does not necessarily mean that they are exaggerated or untrue. They might highlight the deeper, inner meaning of his life and work that was seen only after belief in his resurrection. They were the product of inspired hindsight, or some might even have been given by Christian prophets, speaking in the name of the risen Christ. Whenever these words were spoken, are they true?

d) 'The New Quest'

Bornkamm's work was prompted by a widespread questioning of Bultmann which was initiated by Ernst Kasemann in 1953, with his paper, *The Problem of the Historical Jesus*. Kasemann had argued that it was possible to get behind the *kerygma* to bedrock levels of historical material, though he was only really interested in the sayings of Jesus, and not so much his deeds. This 'New Quest' as it came to be called, sought to find out what was true about Jesus by historical research, divorced from the theology of the Church – there was no room for legitimate theological development and unfolding divine revelation on the part of many of the New Questers.

A further sceptical line of inquiry developed with Trajectory Theory. This stated that later, heretical Christian texts, such as the Gnostic material found at Nag Hammadi, might contain valuable, independent, early material. The New Questers were sceptical about official, early Christian history and saw Christianity in the first two centuries as very diverse and fluid. In *The Gnostic Gospels* Elaine Pagels, for example, who was involved with the team studying the Nag Hammadi texts, argued that Gnosticism was a variant of early Christianity. James M. Robinson was a co-ordinator of this research, and argued for trajectory methodology, too. He was convinced that a good deal of early and probably genuine logia of Jesus were embedded in the *Gospel of Thomas*.

Comparisons between such material reawakened interest in Q as the most primitive layer of tradition in the Synoptics. Its largely wisdom-based collection was seen as the authentic voice of Jesus. (Anything that was different – healings or eschatology – was seen as a later addition. A circular argument?).

There had been a latent anti-Judaism in the work of the New Quest, stripping away anything Jewish about Jesus and looking only for what was original and distinctive. This led to interest in Jesus as a Cynic style philosopher, for they wandered around spouting witty aphorisms, dressed simply, and begged for bread. They had undergone a revival in the first century CE, having had their heyday some centuries earlier when characters such as Diogenes the Athenian wandered around with a lantern in broad daylight searching for an honest man! They carried a simple bag, or pouch, to collect their offerings and this was compared with that mentioned in Jesus' mission speech in Q (e.g. Matthew 10:9–10). There were Cynics in the Hellenised cities of Sepphoris and Tiberias, but we have no evidence that they were active in Galilee proper or that there was a Jewish version of them. Regardless of this, several New Questers, such as the American Jesus Seminar, argue racily that there were. Hand in hand with this is a scepticism about eschatology – Jesus was only interested in the present and not the future. 'The kingdom' is a symbol for existential freedom and practical action to change society.

Scholarly reaction to the more *avant garde* claims of the New Quest, has led to what is often known as a Third Quest, and a renewed interest in first century Judaism and the role of Jesus within it (see the work of Vermes, Sanders et al). This is far more balanced, and avoids the charge of recasting Jesus in the New Questers own image.

5 The Jesus of history

KEY ISSUE There have been reactions to the scepticism of Bultmann and the older, liberal critics. Perrin and Bornkamm, as followers of Bultmann, felt it necessary to anchor faith in the risen Lord in the historical figure of Jesus. It must be the same person who is proclaimed as Lord of the Church.

Perrin formulates three criteria to discern what is historical in the Gospel traditions:

- **Dissimilarity**. If Jesus says anything new and original that cannot be paralleled in the Judaism of his time or in the early Church, then that is likely to be authentic. This is a very severe criterion, for Jesus no doubt shared some ideas with Judaism, and the early Church no doubt taught these things because they were said by Jesus;

- **Multiple attestation.** Themes that are constantly mentioned in the Gospels are likely to be based on fact, e.g. Jesus' concern for the outcasts. However, this does not automatically mean that isolated sayings or events did not happen;
- **Coherence.** If some material coheres with what is revealed about Jesus by the use of the above two criteria, then it might be held to be reliable; this principle is more doubtful than the other two. It is dependent on other material being first substantiated.

Various scholars have reacted against the Bultmann school and think there is a substantial historicity to the Gospels, though the evangelists did feel free to be creative with the material they received and handed on.

- **Dodd**, for example, argues that the outline of events in the Synoptics is the same as that in Peter's sermon in Acts 10:36–43, and that it was the basic shape of the apostolic preaching rather than Mark's invention.
- **Jeremias**, and others, point out that many of the sayings of Jesus can be translated back into Aramaic where they form rhymes, suggesting that they were either the words of Jesus or the products of the very first Jewish Christian communities that were mainly Aramaic-speaking.
- **Vermes** has shown how the miracle stories of Jesus, and his use of 'Abba' in prayer, are part of the lifestyle of the Galilean Hasidim, the charismatic preachers (see Sections 7, 10). There is a strongly Jewish flavour to many of the sayings of Jesus.
- **Lindars** has examined the discourses in John, which are long and theological compared with the short, pithy sayings in the Synoptics. He feels that the longer discourses are based upon shorter sayings which the evangelist has probably developed (so Mark 10:15 or a similar saying lies behind John 3:1–21 and the charge to be born again). There is a clear respect for the Jesus tradition despite the peculiarities of John; and the existence of this tradition is illustrated by passages such as 1 Corinthians 11:23; 15:3 and the various references to the preaching of the apostles in Acts.
- **Gerhardsson** has shown how important oral tradition was in transmitting the teachings of the rabbis in the first century AD; it was said, for example, by Rabbi Ephraim, 'a well-trained pupil is like a well-plastered cistern that loses not a drop.' It is therefore very likely that many of the sayings of Jesus were passed on faithfully in an oral tradition before the Gospels were written, and maybe even afterwards (compare with Papias in the second century saying that he preferred 'living oracles' than things written in books). The evangelists were interested in the basic story of the earthly Jesus, and handed on information about him. Even so, they did reinterpret and create new material if they felt the need to, as Jesus was understood anew after the resurrection, and preached in different contexts. Just how much was handed on, and how much was their creation, is still debated.

As for miracles, some scholars are careful to point out that the historian cannot decide, scientifically and philosophically, whether such things can happen. All they can claim is that they were recorded of Jesus very early in the traditions about him. Also, Bultmann and the earlier liberals have been criticised for holding an outmoded view of science comprising a closed universe of cause and effect with no room for miracles. Modern science postulates a more open universe, where things happen as much by chance as by fixed laws; there is also an interest in the power of the mind over the body, such as the power of faith to heal.

6 Studying the Gospels

KEY ISSUE Scholars have worked out various techniques to dissect and analyse the Gospels, both as finished documents and as clusters of traditions.

a) Source criticism

Matthew and Luke use Mark, but each have original material as well as new material in common. John is an independent tradition. Does an earlier source prove more historically reliable? Can a later source preserve older, oral material?

It was generally assumed that Matthew was the earliest Gospel until recent scholarship has shown that Mark underlies both Matthew and Luke. Matthew is now seen as a development of Mark. There might have been an earlier document connected to Matthew's name, such as a collection of Old Testament proof texts or of some *logia* (sayings) of Jesus, which was worked into Mark's account later (remember Papias and Matthew writing 'the logia in the Hebrew language').

The prologue to Luke admits that many attempts had been made to write down parts of the Gospel tradition (Luke 1:1–3), and there were probably all kinds of logia collections, miracle cycles and Old Testament texts that Jesus was said to have fulfilled, and the Passion narratives. Mark seems to collect material together, such as healing stories, sayings and controversies, and these are fitted into a loose narrative framework, which is based upon that described in Peter's speech in Acts 10:36–43.

Doublets of tradition are explained by using different sources, such as the two feedings in Mark 6:30–44, and Mark 8:1–9. The evangelist had mistakenly seen these as two separate incidents, from two different documents or oral traditions about the same event.

b) Form criticism

Form criticism has two levels. *Gattungsgeschicte* seeks to categorise the literary genres found in the Gospels, breaking them down into logia, parables, miracle stories and so on. *Formgeschichte* then attempts to trace their development before they were written down, in the period of oral tradition. This critical method was pioneered by German scholars such as Schmidt, Dibelius, and Bultmann in between the two world wars. Their work rested upon a number of assumptions :

- The Gospels were folk literature, i.e. being composed orally by telling and retelling over years before being written down.
- A period of oral tradition was assumed, and the possibility of written documents (such as lists of logia, miracle stories) running in parallel to this was not taken seriously. The abiding popularity of oral methods of telling the Gospel story was read into Papias' statement, 'I supposed that things out of books did not profit me so much as the utterances of a voice which lives and abides.'
- The traditions were thought to have circulated independently as units. Preachers recounted them as occasion demanded, and these were eventually collected together as in Mark.

Their most controversial idea was that, in the period of oral transmission, the traditions were moulded and influenced by their **Sitz im Leben**, their life setting. This might have been in the life of Jesus, or in that of the early Church. An example would be the question about paying tax to Caesar (e.g. Mark 12:13–17). Was this really from the Jesus of history, or was it more of a concern for the early Christians? Thus, later ideas would be written back into the Jesus story to meet contemporary needs. The problem is that something actually said by Jesus might have been relevant to later believers in their setting, too. This possibility was played down by the early form critics. They also ignored the Rabbinical tradition of careful training, whereby disciples had to learn oral material faithfully, "like a well-plastered cistern that loses not a drop."

The problem is that much of this is speculation. Classifying the forms of Gospel passages does not necessarily tell us anything about their historicity. Also, a saying that was useful in the early Church, might have actually come from Jesus during his ministry. It was remembered and 'dusted off' at a later time.

c) Redaction criticism

The final form of the text is at issue here. An evangelist is seen to have shaped the material in his own particular way. Thus, an incident in Mark is retold, but with a different emphasis or extra details added. The story of Jesus walking on the water, for example (Mark 6:45–52) is added to in Matthew (Matthew 14:22–33) by having Peter attempting to copy his master. This is seen as Matthew adding themes to do with discipleship.

Scholars such as Bornkamm, Conzelmann and Marxsen pioneered redaction criticism methods as a way of trying to overcome the impasse in form criticism. Too much focus on how the tradition was shaped ignores the impact of its final, literary form. Bornkamm applied redaction criticism to Matthew, Conzelmann to Luke and Marxsen to Mark. The special concerns in each are the theme of discipleship, the delayed *parousia* and the role of the Church, and the interest in Galilee, rather than Jerusalem, as a place of blessing and revelation. Redaction criticism has been popularised in Britain by Norman Perrin, and he saw the impact of work on Luke in particular, for

> Luke the historian becomes a self-conscious theologian, and the details of his composition can be shown convincingly to have been theologically motivated.

Here, he overstates his case, and shows up a danger in redaction criticism methods. Theological meaning does not necessarily mean that a story or detail has been invented. An *actual* event might have a new, theological meaning drawn out of it by the evangelists.

d) Literary criticism

The final form, content and style of the text is considered as an item by itself. Whatever sources or influences, it works as a document, as a story by itself. It was composed that way deliberately to present ideas about Jesus, faith and God. These have an intrinsic value whatever their historical basis. If something is poetic, symbolic, or a later addition, it can still reveal truths.

Literary criticism of the Gospels has focused upon the plot, narrator, structure, characterisation, irony and misunderstandings in the text. A Culpepper's *Anatomy of the Fourth Gospel* uses six basic plot types from literary critic Seymour Chatman, to compare the Gospel with:

- A good hero fails to our moral outrage
- A villain fails and justice is satisfied
- A good hero fails through miscalculation
- A villain wins to the reader's moral outrage
- A good hero wins
- A good hero miscalculates, but after a setback, wins.

Which of these types fits the Fourth Gospel?

M Stibbe also looks at John, in *Readings: John*, using the structuralist analysis. Here a story has a Quest, a Sender, a Receiver of the mission, a Helper, and an Opponent. How does the Fourth Gospel fit this scheme?

e) Canonical criticism

Canonical criticism follows on, very closely, from literary criticism. It stresses the function of the Bible as a whole, as 'canon' (the whole agreed collection of books in Scripture). The New Testament cannot be understood apart from the context of the Old Testament, and a Gospel is part of the whole New Testament. Just as Shakespeare's plays should not be studied in complete isolation from each other, so the Gospels are part of the whole Bible. Here we can see how ideas affect each other and change. There are overarching theological truths and themes, regardless of the actual sources and historicity of episodes. The early Christians responded to Jesus in a certain way, whatever he actually said and did.

f) Sociological criticism

The Gospels (and New Testament) were composed in a particular social setting. Insights about the text can be gleaned by studying this, such as the inclusion of slaves in the church community. This suggests a radical message of God's mercy and grace for all. Hellenistic mystery cults were very elitist, in comparison. Seeing who followed Jesus and who reacted negatively, tells us something about the social order of the day. The influential and powerful were challenged by him, the 'people of the land' – those outside the religious hierarchy – flocked to him.

Sociological study of the Gospels had been taken into the arena of radical politics by John Dominic Crossan in *The Historical Jesus – The Life of a Mediterranean Jewish Peasant.* He argues that the social situation of Galilean villagers was that of near destitution, as all their resources were drained by their Roman overlords, both in taxes and manpower, to run centres such as Sepphoris. Jesus appeared as a radical prophet, overturning tribal and village taboos, and throwing people together in a new community of mutual support. This was the will of God, and the power of God was with him to heal and to feed – practical issues that are a priority for the near destitute. Crossan's work is an impressive cross-cultural study of peasant movements, sociology and revolutionary groups. He uses textual and archaeological evidence from first century Egypt to throw light upon the peasant artisan's lifestyle, with references to contemporaries of Jesus.

Crossan feels that the awesome, charismatic presence of God in Jesus was a jolt that signalled the End, and the hope of a new order. More controversially, he argues that early Christianity did not care about the nature of the Resurrection – the empty tomb and so forth were a later development from the conviction that the God who healed through Jesus was still healing. God was not crucified, and so the movement went on. Some of his evidence is from funerary paintings and inscriptions in the Roman catacombs – images of mother and child, and healing/feeding miracles abound. This ignores the central and primitive belief in some sort of Resurrection that is attested in the earliest Christian Scriptures, and, indeed, some inscriptions, such as appeals for Jesus to save the deceased.

With sociological criticism, our reading of texts can take on a totally new light. Take, for example, Matthew 1 which has the genealogy of Jesus and the story of Joseph's dream. Genealogies were important as social pedigrees; for Jesus to trace ancestry to David was socially powerful for a preacher from Galilee. Joseph's angelic dream reveals his social status, for the common man expected messages from God to come personally through dreams. By contrast, King Herod consulted the scribes with their Scripture scrolls. This was expensive; while each synagogue had scrolls, individuals did not unless they had wealth.

g) Psycho-historical criticism

This is in its infancy and tries to draw a psychological profile of Jesus from various clues in the Gospels. Taking the principle that the child makes the man, deep-seated drives and concerns are outlined in the ministry of Jesus. A central theme seems to be the rejection of his earthly family for a wider community, his sense of acceptance by God as Father, and his fathering of the lost, the 'people of the land.' There is also a rejection of power and many contemporary models of Messiahship.

7 Jesus the Jew

KEY ISSUE Recent scholarship has stressed that, behind all the debates of Gospel historicity, we must remember the Jewishness of Jesus and fit him into the culture of his day.

A breakthrough in this debate was Geza Vermes' *Jesus the Jew,* first published in 1973. He sifts the Gospel traditions and points out details and parallels from the Judaism of the time. His motive is to present a fresh vision of Jesus for Jews and Christians alike:

> ... if, after working his way through the book, the reader recognises that this man, so distorted by Christian and Jewish myth alike ... Some small beginning may have been made in the repayment to him of a debt long overdue.
>
> *Jesus the Jew* (1973), p. 17

His most striking contribution is to compare Jesus with Galilean holy men, *hasidim* (pious ones) such as Hanina Ben Dosa and Honi the

Circle-drawer. These were individuals who sometimes performed cures, had a close relationship to God, sometimes calling him 'Abba', and were approachable by the common people, outside the religious hierarchy.

Jewish scholars have been concerned to reclaim Jesus as their own, seeing a primitive kernel of historical tradition behind the Gospels. Dan Cohn-Sherbok in *The Jewish Heritage*, can claim:

> Jesus of Nazareth spent most of his life in Galilee where he acted as a healer, exorcist and itinerant preacher who proclaimed the imminent arrival of the Kingdom of God. After a brief association with John the Baptist, he attracted disciples from among the most marginalised sectors of society ...

An original turn of research is found in Bruce Chilton and Jacob Neusner's *Judaism in the New Testament.* They argue that Christianity, in the New Testament phase of development, was simply one type of Judaism amongst many. After the fall of Jerusalem in AD 70, the form of rabbinic Judaism that took precedence was only one strand before the Roman victory. There were philosophical movements, Messianic sects such as the Essenes, wild, apocalyptic speculation, theological reactionaries like the Sadducees as well as the movement with scribes and rabbis. Early Christianity was just another strand, a Messianic sect proclaiming the resurrection of their Master and the imminent end of the world. They criticise scholars, such as Sanders, who write about Judaism in the first century AD as though it was a unity:

> How Philo will have understood the Dead Sea Scrolls, or the authors of apocalyptic writings will have understood those of the Mishnah ... we are never told.

John Dominic Crossan writes, in *The Historical Jesus – the Life of a Mediterranean Jewish Peasant*:

> By the end of the first century two great religions, rabbinic Judaism and early Christianity, were emerging from a common matrix. Each claimed to be its only legitimate continuation, and each had texts and traditions to prove that claim. Each, in fact, represented an equally valid, equally surprising, and equally magnificent leap out of the past and into the future. It would, in truth, be difficult to say, had Moses awoke from slumber around 200 CE, which of the two would have surprised him the more ...

The turning point came much later, when Jesus was seen to have replaced the Torah, and set aside the ritual laws totally. Early Jewish Christians blended the old and the new to some extent, worshipping in the Temple and synagogue. Rabbinic, post-AD 70 Judaism rejected Christianity as a valid stream of Judaism, though Chilton and

Neusner go a long way to open up the case. Even doctrines such as the incarnation of God in Jesus can be understood in a context of Judaism. A common hope for the Jew is the dwelling of God with his creation in a restored harmony. The Jewish biblical commentary, *Genesis Rabbah* states:

> If there are no disciples, there will be no sages. If there are no sages, there will be no prophets. If there are no prophets, the Holy One, blessed be he, will not allow his presence to come to rest in the world.

The message that this presence came to rest so intimately and profoundly in the life of one man might have been more congenial if not for mutual suspicions and horrific persecutions of Jews by the Church through the Middle Ages and beyond.

8 Jesus outside the Gospels

KEY ISSUE Jesus is mentioned a few times by Jewish and pagan writers.

a) Cornelius Tacitus

Tacitus wrote the *Annals*, a history of the Roman Empire from AD 14–68. Unfortunately, the first part of the work has not survived, which might have dealt with the trial of Jesus. Jesus is mentioned in the account of Nero's reign and the outbreak of the great fire of Rome in AD 64. The Christians, we are told:

> got their name from Christ, who was executed by sentence of the procurator Pontius Pilate in the reign of Tiberius. The pernicious superstition, suppressed for the moment, broke out again, not only throughout Judaea, the birthplace of the plague, but also in the city of Rome …
>
> *Annals* 15:44

This brief mention affirms Jesus' real existence when Pilate was in Judaea, and Tiberius was Emperor. This fits the New Testament chronology.

b) Pliny the Younger

Pliny was governor of Bithynia in Asia Minor from AD 111–113. He wrote to the Emperor Trajan, mentioning the Christians:

> They meet on a certain fixed day before sunrise and sing an antiphonal hymn to Christ as a god, and bind themselves with an oath: not to

> commit any crime, but to abstain from all acts of theft, robbery and adultery, and from breaches of trust ...
>
> *Letter* 10:96

We have no details about the life of Jesus here, except the fact that Jesus was worshipped as divine by the early second century AD.

c) Suetonius

Suetonius wrote *c.* AD 120 about the reign of Claudius:

> He expelled the Jews from Rome because of the riots they were causing at the instigation of Chrestus.
>
> *Claud* 25.4

'Chrestus' is probably a variant of 'Christus'. This reflects early Christian/Jewish tensions, but tells us nothing about the life of Jesus.

d) Lucian

The satirist Lucian of Samosata mentioned that Christians:

> worship that crucified sage of theirs and live according to his laws.
>
> *Peregrinus* 11

e) Josephus

Josephus was a Jew who lived from ad 37 to *c.* 100 AD. He was involved in the Jewish uprising against Rome in 66 AD and was taken prisoner. He changed sides, honouring the Romans for their civilisation. His *Jewish Antiquities* was written to show how cultured his own people were. The following was written in about AD 93–94; besides a lengthy section on John the Baptist, he also mentions Jesus:

> About this time lived Jesus, a wise man (*if indeed one ought to refer to him as a man*). For he was one who did surprising deeds, a teacher of those who delight in accepting the unusual. He brought trouble to many Jews, and also many from the Greek world. (*He was the Messiah-Christ.*) On the accusation of our leading men Pilate condemned him to the cross, but those who had loved him from the first did not cease to do so. (*For on the third day he appeared to them again alive, just as the divine prophets had spoken about these and countless other marvellous things about him.*) And to this day the tribe of Christians, named after him, has not died out.

The sections placed in brackets and italics were probably added by a Christian monk in the later copies that we have. Once removed, the rest of the text could well have been written by a first century Jew.

f) The Mishnah and Talmuds

This is a collection of Jewish laws from about AD 200. Set alongside these were commentaries containing stories of various rabbis. One of these has the details that:

> On the eve of Passover Yeshu was hanged. For forty days before the execution took place, a herald went forth and cried, 'He is going forth to be stoned because he has practised sorcery and enticed and led Israel astray'
>
> b.Sanh. 43a

Yeshu is Jesus; 'hanged' means crucified. The penalty of stoning was given to blasphemers, though the Romans dispensed justice by crucifixion. The charge of sorcery might be a hint that Jesus worked miracles (see Matthew 12: 22–24).

g) Mara Bar Serapion

Mara Bar Serapion was a Syrian Stoic philosopher who wrote to his son from prison. Serapion was from Samosata. This letter might date as early as AD 73, and he complains that the wise are often rejected, with tribulation being sent upon the people afterwards as a punishment. So, the people of Athens killed Socrates, and famine followed; the Samians killed Pythagoras, and their land was buried in sand:

> or what did it avail the Jews to kill their wise king, since their kingdom was taken away from them from that time on?

The 'wise king' is a reference to Jesus, and the second part of the extract refers to the events of AD 70 and the fall of Jerusalem. Serapion was attracted to the teaching of Christ, though still a pagan. He adds that the wise men he mentions are not lost forever, but something of their work lives on, 'Nor is the wise king, because of the new law which he has given.' Interestingly, this author lived in the region that produced Matthew, a gospel that is concerned with the Kingship of Jesus and his new Law.

h) Thallus

Thallus wrote a three-volume history which has been lost, though he is mentioned by various writers. Julius Africanus (*c.* AD 170–240) mentions that Thallus had tried to explain the darkness that attended the crucifixion as an eclipse. Thallus was writing sometime after AD 52, and might have mentioned Jesus fairly early in the first century.

Summary List

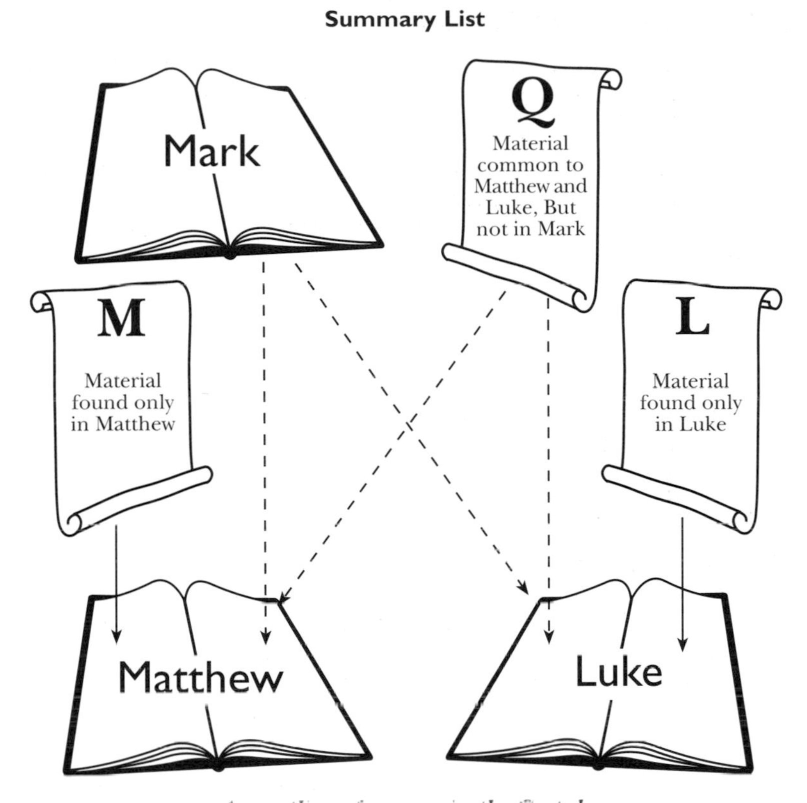

An outline of sources in the Gospels

- The Gospels are not biographies. They are interpretative preaching works. The Jesus story was reworked and interpreted after the resurrection. Scholars ask how much order and sequence was imposed on floating units of tradition (stories and logia) by the evangelists.
- Attempts to write an accurate historical life of Jesus are doomed to failure by gaps in our knowledge, the levels of interpretation present, and the presuppositions of modern authors. The nineteenth-century lives of Jesus displayed the prejudices of their authors (e.g. rejecting the miraculous).
- Bultmann sidestepped the issue by separating the **Christ of faith** from the **Jesus of history**. He was radically sceptical about the historicity of the Gospels and argued that what mattered was faith in the nature of the risen Christ and inner change in the believer.
- 'The New Quest' (an attempt to reclaim some historic content in the Gospels) reacted against Bultmann's scepticism and saw a continuity between Jesus and Christ. Various techniques were used to trace historical aspects:

- Perrin's triple criteria
- Lindars' parallels of Johannine discourses with Synoptic logia
- Jeremias and **Aramaisms**
- Gerhardsson and the reliability of the oral tradition
- Dodd and the similar structure of the apostolic *kerygma* with the sequence of the Synoptics.

- Various forms of criticism have stripped the Gospels down but cannot really comment on the historical question:
  - Source criticism (the sources used by the evangelists)
  - Form criticism (the shape of units in the oral period)
  - Redaction criticism (the role of the evangelist as editor)
  - Literary criticism (the final form of the text as a work of art)
  - Sociological criticism (the social issues traced in Gospel passages).
- The Jewishness of Jesus has been the focus of recent studies, placing Jesus firmly in the first century as a man of his time. Judaism before AD 70 was a diverse and fluid movement. The historical existence of the man Jesus is attested in several extra-Biblical authors in the early centuries of the Christian era.

Answering structured and essay questions on Chapter 8

1. Do you think Bultmann was justified in his use of 2 Corinthians 5:16 ('... even though we once knew Christ from a human point of view, we know him no longer in that way')?
2. In what way did Bornkamm think that the Gospel traditions were 'brim full of history'?
3. Can deep and inner meanings of someone's life and teaching be discerned after their lifetime? When applied to Jesus, does this make some insights in the Gospel less true?
4. Read Mark 8:31–33. There are three possible points of view about the historicity of this passage:
   - It is completely historical, reflecting Jesus' own understanding
   - It is completely unhistorical, being made up by the early Church
   - It is partly historical, being a development of an idea or saying of Jesus.

   Explain why the early Church might have invented this material. Also, if it is based upon an actual saying of Jesus that has been developed, what might that have been about?
5. List the outline of Jesus' ministry that is in Acts 10:36–43. Compare this with Mark's outline of events.
6. Lindars feels that the lengthy discourses in John might be based upon shorter logia in the Synoptics. Match up these Synoptic passages with the verses from John:
   Luke15:3–7; Mark 8:38; Matthew 9:9; Mark 9:33–37; Mark 10:13–16
   John 3:1–7; John 10:1–18; John 14:1–11.
7. Read through Mark 2 and try to classify the forms or types of material as you think best.

8. Some would explain the *Sitz im Leben* of Mark 2:18–20 as the life and worship of the early Church, when it was separating itself from Jewish customs. Why might they think this?
9. Compare the incident of walking on the water in Mark 6:45–52 and Matthew 14:22–33. What emphasis does each evangelist bring to the story?
10. Read these NT texts: Matthew 11:4-5; Mark 2:17; Galatians 3:28. How do these reveal that Jesus was socially inclusive?

9 The Death of Jesus

KEYWORDS

apotheosis – being taken to the gods and granted immortality

atonement – reconciliation with God

expiation – taking away guilt

pharmakos – the Hellenistic scapegoat custom, where a person was driven out of a city or killed each year

propitiation – appeasing someone's anger

Sanhedrin – the Council of Jewish elders

scapegoat – the OT custom of transferring the sins of the people onto a goat and driving it into the wilderness

Suffering Servant – the anonymous character in Isaiah 53 who suffers for the sins of the people

1 Introduction

KEY ISSUE 'No human death has influenced and shaped the world of late antiquity, and indeed the history of mankind as a whole down to the present day, more than that of the Galilean craftsman and itinerant preacher who was crucified before the gates of Jerusalem in AD 30 as a rebel and messianic pretender.' Martin Hengel in *The Atonement.*

The Romans crucified thousands of people, and there were 'messianic pretenders' before and after Jesus of Nazareth. His death should have been the end of the Jesus movement, as all his followers' hopes were dashed. Yet, history was very different. This chapter will survey the issues, beginning with the historical questions surrounding the trial and execution of Jesus, and then the mythical/spiritual aspects will be addressed.

2 The trial and execution of Jesus

a) The Passion narrative

The four Gospels narrate the same, basic story. This can be set out as follows:

- Arrest
- Peter's denial
- Jesus before High Priest/Sanhedrin
- Handing over to Pilate
- Hearing before Pilate
- Offer to release Barabbas or Jesus (missing from John)
- Condemnation of Jesus (missing from John)
- Mocking of Jesus (missing from Luke and John)
- Journey to the cross (missing from John)
- Crucifixion
- Mockery of the crucified Jesus (missing from John)
- Two thieves (missing from Luke and John)
- Death of Jesus

The Gospel tradition has three groups of people involved – the Jewish aristocracy, the Romans and the people. The penalty of crucifixion was a Roman punishment for robbers and rebels; to what extent were the other groups implicated, and why? Jeremias asks, 'How could Jesus have been brought to the cross by people who were blessed by his signs and wonders?' How far was his death politically or theologically motivated, and what made some of the people turn against him?

The Jewish leaders did not have the power to enact a death sentence (the *ius gladii*) – this was in the hands of the Roman prefect and had been since the advent of direct Roman rule. The **Sanhedrin** would only have been able to recommend a death sentence for blasphemy. (The only exceptions to this, such as the stoning of Stephen in Acts 6–7, would have been when the prefect was away or there was a gap before the appointment of a new prefect.) The accounts of Jesus before the Jewish leaders are complicated and conflicting.

- *Mark 14:53–65* implies that Jesus was taken straight to the high priest (presumably Annas) who assembled the Sanhedrin in the middle of the night.
- *Matthew 26:57–68* says that Jesus was taken to the house of Caiaphas first. (Caiaphas was the former high priest, and still held that office's respect, a 'high priest emeritus') and the Sanhedrin gathered there.
- *Luke 22:66–71* has Jesus taken to 'the high priest's house' (unnamed) and held until daybreak, when the Sanhedrin meets.
- *John 18:13–24* has Jesus taken to Annas, where he is questioned by the high priest, alone. Then he is sent to Caiaphas. There is no account of what transpires there.

The charges brought against him in these trials (Matthew/Mark) or interrogations (Luke/John) vary. The trial tradition has two charges – speaking against the Temple and claiming to be the Messiah.

- **Speaking against the Temple** This charge referred to Jesus' prophecies about the Temple's destruction and could have carried a death penalty for blasphemy. Gentiles straying into the inner courts were threatened with death – 'he will have himself to blame that his death ensues'. Perhaps a sense of community justice could extend beyond this to Jews who slandered the Temple, as with Stephen's martyrdom. The Jewish aristocracy were dependent upon revenues from the Temple, too, and would have moved to silence any threat to this, as they did with another prophecy against the Temple from one Jesus son of Ananias, as reported by Josephus.
- **Claiming to be the Messiah** The Messianic claim, combining the three titles of 'Messiah', 'Son' and 'Son of Man', would not have carried a death penalty – many claimed to be the Messiah. This would have unnerved the Jewish aristocracy as it was a political threat.

The interrogation tradition centres on the supposed Messiahship of Jesus, and it is interesting that the charge becomes political when he is handed over to Pilate. In Luke 23:2 the charge becomes political agitation and refusal to pay taxes. John also has underlying political motives for handing Jesus over (see John 11:47–53).

The nocturnal trial was against the conditions for capital trials laid dawn in the Mishnah, and a death sentence could not have been imposed until the second day of the trial. Of course, the events might predate the traditions that were later codified in the Mishnah – Sadducean law was harsher than Pharisaic law which became the norm, later. (It is worth noting that the Talmud has the tradition that Jesus was sentenced to be stoned for blasphemy for practising sorcery and leading Israel astray – perhaps an echo of the deliberations with the Sanhedrin?)

Whatever the exact sequence of events, Jesus was taken to representatives of the Jewish leaders before being handed over to the Romans. John suggests that there was collaboration during the arrest – John 18:3 has a detachment of Roman soldiers with the Temple guards being sent to arrest Jesus.

The people are implicated to greater or lesser degrees by the different Gospels – Matthew has them bringing a curse upon themselves, 'his blood be upon us and upon our children', (Matthew 27:25) referring to the destruction of Jerusalem. Luke has some in the crowd weeping and pleading for Jesus (Like 23:13–27) including many women. The tradition of the two thieves, one rejecting and one accepting Christ, reflects this sensitivity, too.

A motive for the crowd's behaviour could be disillusionment with the failure of Jesus to start an uprising after the cleansing of the Temple. Barabbas, on the other hand, was a rebel who would 'get his hands dirty' and fight. There is no evidence of a Passover custom of releasing a prisoner, and it is odd that this is not mentioned in Josephus. However, occasional amnesties are attested in other parts of the Empire such as Egypt, where a criminal is handed over with the words, 'You deserved to be flogged ... but I will give you to the crowd'. The Barabbas-Jesus offer could have been a one-off event, inspired by the circumstances, and a contrivance of Pilate's to exonerate himself from the guilt of killing an innocent man.

The Roman involvement is played down in some of the sources as the early Christians were trying to exonerate themselves before the Roman authorities. The M material in Matthew has the tradition of Pilate's wife's dream (Matthew 27:19). In the L material in Luke, two rulers, Herod and Pilate, attest the innocence of Jesus. This is implied in John where Jesus claims, 'He who delivered me to you has the greater sin'. (John 19:11) referring to the Jewish authorities. Whatever theological reservations the Sanhedrin held about Jesus, the clearest tradition to emerge from all the conflicting evidence is that Jesus was a political threat, and he would also have been viewed with great suspicion by Rome. Sadly, later traditions heaped more and more blame upon the Jews (as a race) and led to persecutions and prejudice for years to come. Pilate's confrontation with Jesus is best understood as *coercitio,* a compulsory measure, rather than *cognito,* a formal trial according to rules of the law. A Roman prefect was empowered to take whatever measures he deemed necessary to keep the peace.

3 Old Testament influences in the Passion narrative

KEY ISSUE Certain details in the Passion Narratives in the Gospels can be linked to OT references or prophecies.

The evangelists were trying to claim that details of Christ's treatment were fulfilling Scripture. Psalm 22 was a major influence. This was often recited by martyrs. Isaiah 53, the '**Suffering Servant**' passage, was another. Some would argue that such passages have been deliberately worked into the story, inventing scenes to fit details from the OT. This is, of course, a circular argument, and all that can be said with certainty is that these passages show what links the early Christians made with OT passages, and how these were used in a Messianic sense by them.

4 Why did Judas betray Jesus?

This question has exercised exegetes for years. The superficial answer is for greed. The price he was paid was relatively small, though, being a price of a slave. If the motive was greed, then why the remorse that led to suicide?

William Klassen in *Judas – Betrayer or Friend of Jesus?* argues that Judas has been caricatured and demonised in later tradition. The verb *paradidomi* in Greek means 'to hand over' and cannot really bear the meaning of 'betray' in the NT or in Classical literature. Furthermore, he does not see Judas as beyond the grace of God. Surely, the prayer of Christ on the cross to forgive his enemies, should extend to Judas? Klassen traces a disturbing tendency to firm up the boundaries of who is in the Church and who is outside it in rewriting the figure of Judas as a character in a morality play, or a pantomime villain who evokes hisses and booing. Klassen speculates that Judas might have had access to the Temple hierarchy, and could have been a go-between for Jesus and the high priest. In this sense he was an 'informer' (Hebrew: **mesira**). Perhaps Judas believed that Jesus should confront the high priest, face to face, and that his rebuke would bring repentance and speed up the dawn of the Kingdom of God. Judas acted innocently, and upon the orders of Jesus. Perhaps, at the end, Jesus was realising that this encounter would result in his martyrdom, a fact which he only half eluded to, or kept from his disciple, Judas. The failure of the arrangement and the death of his Master, would have brought on the agonising remorse that made Judas take his own life.

This is all plausible, though we simply do not have enough evidence to decide the matter. Another idea is that Judas was forcing Jesus' hand to call for an uprising, or to bring in the Kingdom by cornering the disciples in the Garden of Gethsemane. It would have been 'now or never'. Jesus' refusal to fight and his subsequent death backfired upon Judas, who genuinely loved his Master. This picture demands that Judas was a Zealot, and some have seen a reference in his name to the Sicarii, assassins who killed Romans in the crowd with daggers.

5 The saving significance of Jesus' death

KEY ISSUE The New Testament sees his death as a sacrifice. Jesus offers himself, willingly, in an act of self-giving love.

This has various interpretations put upon it, drawing upon OT scripture and the sacrificial cult of the day. An early text that was used to understand the death of the Messiah was Isaiah 53, a strange poem about the anonymous servant of Yahweh, which forms part of the Servant Song collection in the works of the prophet. Only on one occasion is the Servant identified with Israel (Isaiah 49:3) and various suggestions to identify the figure with a righteous king, priest, or prophet do not fit. In Isaiah 53, the servant suffers, offering himself without any dispute, and he **atones** for the sins of the people

(Isaiah 53:4–5). It is a moot point whether Jesus ever identified himself with this figure. This is implied in his predictions of the passion, such as Mark 10:32–34, but these could have been placed upon his lips by the early Church.

One logion of Jesus says, 'For the Son of Man came not to be served but to serve, and to give his life a ransom for many.' (Mark 10:45). Isaiah 53 and, possibly Daniel 11:33–35, lie behind this. Schweitzer believed that Jesus gave himself up, thinking that his sufferings would bring the Kingdom of God to birth after the 'Messianic woes'.

Paul could state that the death was a reconciling act between humanity and God: 'that is, in Christ, God was reconciling the world to himself ...'(2 Corinthians 5:19).

Before surveying the various strands of NT interpretation of the death, it is necessary to set the cultural scene by examining attitudes to martyrs and heroes in the ancient world.

a) The Hellenistic world

The death of the righteous philosopher is seen, par excellence, in the account of the death of Socrates. He felt the command of an inner voice to seek and speak the truth, and he looked death fearlessly in the face:

> ... But I suppose I am allowed, or rather bound, to pray the gods that my removal from this world to the other may be prosperous. This is my prayer, then; and I hope that it may be granted.' With these words, quite calmly and with no sign of distaste, he drained the cup in one breath ...
>
> Plato, *Phaedo*

Hermias, a friend of Aristotle, was executed by Alexander. Aristotle declared, 'The Muses will make you immortal'. The Cynic philosopher Peregrinus Proteus leaped upon a funeral pyre to demonstrate that he was not afraid of death. Lucian's account explains that he did this for the welfare of humanity, to teach them not to fear for their immortal souls.

The Hellenistic world knew a long, ancient tradition of self-sacrifice for the beloved, for friends, family or city. Creon died to save his city, 'I am going, and will deliver the city, and I will give up my life to die for this land'. The idea that the heroes, kings, or warriors died for their people had cultic and religious overtones.

This 'dying for' sometimes had atoning significance. Clement of Rome refers to this tradition:

> Many kings and rulers, when a time of pestilence has set in, have followed the counsel of oracles, and given themselves up to death, that they might rescue their subjects through their own blood.

These deaths were self-offerings, being divinely directed. Early traditions spoke of the death of Menoeceus atoning for the guilt of Oedipus, or of Polyxena's sacrifice releasing the spirit of Achilles. The plays of Euripides have a fixation with this concept, with the deaths of his heroes being enacted with details of the sacrificial cult of the temples. The most striking account is in the *Bacchae* with the death of Pentheus when he is lead from Thebes by Dionysus and torn to pieces by the ecstatic women. His death is a punishment for denying worship to the god, and Thebes is spared by his **expiatory** death.

Ancient lore declared that the martyrs were honoured by the gods with immortality ('**apotheosis**'). The spirit of Achilles is carried to the gods, and, in Pindar, he is the judge of the dead. In other poets, he is venerated as a god in Elysium. Heracles was carried to Olympus from his funeral pyre, and in Euripides' *Alkestis*, he descends into Hades, fights the forces of darkness, and brings forth the spirit of Alkestis – 'I joined a struggle with the Lord of spirits', i.e. Death. In ancient Tarsus, Heracles was venerated as a saviour god. In later times, all who died heroic deaths were treated as demigods.

A final point is the existence of the ***pharmakos*** tradition. This was the Greek version of the **scapegoat**. A condemned criminal, or an undesirable (sadly, often a disabled person) was paraded around the city, cursed, and then either driven out or put to death. In Rhodes, for example, a criminal was put to death outside the city gates in front of the temple of Artemis. This action was thought to purify the city and avert the wrath of the gods.

b) Jewish traditions

Judaism knew no veneration of the heroes and the martyrs, for its fierce monotheism forbade it. Honouring the spirits of the dead, or calling upon them was also forbidden (see 1 Samuel 28 and the witch of Endor). It is only in later texts, composed under a degree of Hellenistic influence, that the idea of the martyr's sacrifice emerges. Daniel 11:33–35 speaks of some of the wise being purified by their suffering, and Daniel 12:2 offers them the hope of resurrection. 2 Maccabees 6–7 catalogue the sufferings of zealous martyrs. Their sufferings are punishment for the sins of the people, and are necessary to bring God's wrath to an end quickly; 'these punishments were designed not to destroy but to discipline our people'. (2 Maccabees 6:12b). In a limited manner, these deaths could be said to be atoning.

c) The Hellenistic sacrificial cult

There were various types of sacrifice:

- Votive offerings – objects are offered to the gods to ask for their help. In Homer, these offerings were like bargains, negotiating with the god.

- Festivals – at a city's great festivals, sacrifices would be offered in praise and thanksgiving to the appropriate gods. Only a portion of the meat would be offered upon the altar. The rest would be eaten by the family group, in a feast.
- Aversion sacrifices – sacrifices of animals, made to avert harm from evil powers, the spirits of the dead, or the gods of the Underworld, were either burned whole or buried. These rites were performed with fear and terror.
- Placatory sacrifices – the Olympian deities were sometimes offered a sacrifice to placate their anger.
- Communion sacrifices – This is the idea that eating sacrificial meat helped the worshippers share the blessing of the god. The clearest example of this was with the worshippers of Dionysus. They wandered the hills, tearing at the flesh of a bull, believing that they were eating the god himself. It is possible that this also occurred in the rites of initiation into the cult of Mithras. The initiate was stood underneath a platform where a bull was slaughtered, so that the blood dripped over him. At some point, a cup was shared, and this was either of actual blood, or of wine as a symbol of blood. Whether the cup was a simple gesture of fellowship upon being initiated, or a means of initiation by communing with the god, is debated.

The philosophers criticised aspects of the sacrificial cult. They rejected any notion of bribe, and argued that an offering was only acceptable if it was a thank offering. Sacrifice was tolerated as a part of public religion and order, but the concept of the 'reasonable sacrifice' of living a virtuous life developed. Plato, in the *Phaedro*, argues that there is an inseparable connection between virtue and piety.

Various schools of thought which stressed the unchanging nature of the gods, or God, saw no utility in sacrifice, for the divine could not be influenced. However, offering sacrifice might be good for the worshipper. It might not affect the gods but, by giving up something costly, it might heal our own evil. Belief in Fate in the later Hellenistic period also downplayed the role of sacrifice.

Yet, opposition to the Christian refusal to sacrifice to the Emperor united the many schools as the Emperor Cult was good for the social order. Some excused this by saying that lesser deities could be influenced by sacrifice. Only Porphry, of the Neo-Platonist school, refused to sacrifice animals, seeing the taking of their life as immoral, but other offerings could be substituted, and the Hermetic writings opposed all sacrifice apart from the 'reasonable sacrifice'.

d) The Jewish sacrificial cult

Jewish sacrifice could be categorised into three types: communion sacrifices; holocausts; expiatory sacrifices. These can be found, for example, in Leviticus 4.

i) Communion sacrifices
This meant, as with the Greek custom, most of the meat was eaten by the worshippers, some by the priest, and some offered on the altar. Before the Temple was built in Jerusalem, this happened at local altars whenever meat was eaten. These became less important to Diaspora Jews who could not get to the Temple very often.

ii) Holocausts
This was a whole burnt offering as an act of pure worship, giving something up totally to Yahweh. There was no idea of this averting evil, as in the Hellenistic world. It is interesting that fasting took the place of these offerings after the destruction of the Temple in AD 70.

iii) Expiatory sacrifice
Part of the offering was placed upon the altar, and the rest was eaten by the priests and not by the worshipper, for it was for his/her purification. The blood ritual was more elaborate, with pourings and sprinklings; the shedding of blood was seen to be the efficacious agent in expiating sin for, as many ancient people believed, the life-force was thought to reside in the blood: 'For the life of the flesh is in the blood' (Lev 7:11). **'Expiation'** means 'taking away', and is not to be confused with **'propitiation'**, which means 'appeasing'. Yahweh was not to be appeased, but sin was to be taken away or covered. This means that the sacrifice was more for the benefit of the worshipper; it did not change God's nature.

iv) Passover
Two other forms of sacrifice are to be found in the Passover meal and the Day of Atonement. The sacrificial lamb was a reminder of the aversion of evil, as the destroying angel passed over the houses daubed with the sacrificial blood. With the central Temple, the Passover became a national pilgrimage rather than a local, family meal. The blood was no longer daubed on doorposts, but was poured out at the base of the altar. In modern day Judaism, the sacrifice of the animal has been lost, and it is a memorial meal and a thanksgiving.

v) The Day of Atonement
This contained very primitive rituals in early Judaism. Two expiatory sacrifices were offered – a bull for the priests and a goat for the people. Then, a second goat was taken to the high priest who laid his hands upon its head and confessed the sins of the people – thus it became the scapegoat. The sins of the people were transferred to it, and it was driven out into the wilderness. An obscure reference is made to averting evil from Azazel, a demonic power (see Leviticus 16:8–10).

Jewish sacrifice retained primitive aspects, with language that suggested that early sacrifices were thought to provide food for Yahweh, but this notion was lost as their lofty idea of God demythologised this. There are few tirades against this old notion, for there did not need to be (but see Psalm 50). The attacks on sacrifice from the prophets are against ideas of bribery, that the rich can offer fine offerings and have their sins ignored.

The sacrifice of Jesus was expounded against the above backgrounds. A total thank offering, a total expiatory offering, a total aversion against evil, was offered in his death on the cross. This theology is systematically presented in Hebrews. In Hebrews 10, the once-for-all sacrifice of Jesus replaces the whole OT cult:

> And it is by God's will that we have been sanctified through the offering of the body of Jesus Christ once for all.
>
> *Hebrews 10:10*

> Therefore, my friends, since we have confidence to enter the sanctuary by the blood of Jesus, by the new and living way that he opened for us through the curtain (that is, through his flesh) ...
>
> *Hebrews 10:19*

Just as all other images of deliverance, salvation and eschatological fulfilment were focused in Jesus, so too was the whole apparatus of atonement. His death was believed to bring perfect forgiveness and was a perfect offering of obedience to the Father – 'a fragrant offering and sacrifice to God' (Eph 5:2b).

Also, the partial atonement wrought by the deaths of worthy men and women in Hellenistic tales, and the zealous Jews in the Maccabean times, was a total atonement in the case of the death of Jesus. The early Christians worshipped at the Temple, but the only evidence that they still sacrificed is limited to instances of votive offerings, when making vows, such as Paul in Acts 21:23–26. The Passover itself was now the Eucharist, with the sacrifice of Christ replacing that of the lamb. They could offer, also, a 'reasonable sacrifice' of their lives and their praise, as in the more refined Hellenistic movements (see Romans 12:1). The idea of averting evil in the Passover and in the scapegoat, as well as the pagan practices, came to the fore in the idea of defeating the Devil (Hebrews 2:14–15; 1 John 3:8; Revelation 20). This is a minor theme in the NT, though, and it takes a more original turn in Paul's writings. Here, he uses the language of the slave market, whereby the believer had been ransomed, or bought. The former slave master was often seen as the Devil by the Church Fathers, but in the Pauline writings it was the impersonal power of sin, brought to life by the demands of the Law, the whole moral and ritual burden of the OT. Paul agreed that the Torah was just and righteous, but it proved to be an impossible burden when you tried to follow it. If you tried to follow all its precepts with a perfectionist mentality, then you were bound to fail, and Paul had such scruples, as revealed in passages such as Romans 7. The righteous Law only made you feel worse; it awakened your sense of sin, of failure.

> For we know that the law is spiritual: but I am of the flesh, sold into slavery under sin.
>
> *Romans 7:14*

Christ's death was representative, and he both lived the demands of the Law, and had taken the punishment for human failure.

> Christ redeemed us from the curse of the law by becoming a curse for us ...
>
> *Galatians 3:13*

Conversely, in his death the believer died (through baptism) and rose again. The new life was in the power of the Spirit. Possessing the Spirit meant that the believer would be transformed within, no longer under the demands of the Law and the whims of 'the flesh':

> And those who belong to Christ Jesus have crucified the flesh with its passions and desires. If we live by the Spirit, let us also be guided by the Spirit.
>
> *Galatians 5:24*

Paul's idea of Christ becoming a curse was linked with an original way of reading Deuteronomy 21:23: 'Cursed is everyone who is hanged on a tree'.

The cross was linked with 'the tree', but this was slightly out of context. The Deuteronomy verse concerned the practice of hanging executed criminals out on a tree for all to see. Crucifixion was the actual means of execution. There is no known parallel usage of Deuteronomy, linking this with crucifixion in the Rabbinic sources or literature of the period. In fact, the late rabbis argued that capital punishment was a means of expiation for the criminal (Tosefta, Sanhedrin 9:5). Other rabbis took the Deuteronomy verse as applying a curse to those who did the hanging, and not the victim themselves. Only the Temple Scroll from the Qumran Community takes the view that a curse was attached *to the victim* if the hanging was prolonged, and the victim was exposed overnight. Of course, the Rabbinical writings were later, and first century Judaism was a mix of many styles and positions. We do not have enough evidence to conclude that Paul was being original in his use of Deuteronomy 21:23, but he certainly was in applying it to the Messiah, in the sense of the Suffering Servant in Isaiah 53.

There is also an implicit idea of a suffering God. *God* was *in* Christ reconciling the world to himself (2 Cor 5:19) and a high priest who has been tested like us also echoes this divine empathy with the human condition (Heb 4:15). This theme has become the most vibrant manner of understanding the cross in contemporary Christianity. People in the past were just as capable of barbarism as those in modern Kosovo or Rwanda, but we have multi-media communications to beam images and news around the world so that we are aware of most things that go horribly wrong. Jürgen Moltmann developed this theme par excellence in his *The Crucified God*, SCM (1974), after his experiences in the Second World War. The divine empathy, identifying with suffering humanity, is representative and inclusive – all suffer and die in him, and rise in him. God himself has a story and a history, both in his inner life, and in his involvement in the world:

> All human history, however much it may be determined by guilt and death, is taken up into this 'history of God', i.e. into the Trinity, and integrated into the future of the 'history of God'. There is no suffering which in this history of God is not God's suffering; no death which has not been God's death in the history of Golgotha ...

Behind all the metaphors for understanding the saving significance of Christ's death is the basic notion of self-giving love. The cross was an acted parable of the love of God – see John 3:16; 15:13; Romans 5:8; 1 John 4:9. The sacrificial cult and the language of the slave market might seem far away and alien to modern readers, but it was a relevant first-century way of explaining the reconciling love shown on the cross.

Summary List

Ways of explaining the saving power of the cross:

- **Full atonement** – Jesus fulfilled all the expiation sacrifices of the Temple cult, and also of the martyr tradition that had grown up since the time of the Maccabees.
- **Perfect offering** – Jesus offered a perfect life of obedience to God, fulfilling the idea of offering something costly, or of 'reasonable worship'.
- **Aversion of evil** – Jesus had defeated the Devil, and was the new scapegoat and Lamb of God.
- **Communion** – Jesus offered his followers participation in a communion sacrifice which remembered his sacrifice on the cross – the Eucharist.
- **Slave redemption** – Jesus had bought the sinner out of slavery to sin and the demands of the Torah.
- **Divine empathy** – Jesus revealed a God who suffered in and with his creation.
- **Token of love** – The cross was an acted parable of the self-giving love of God.

The Passion narrative follows a similar form and sequence in the Gospels, with slight deviations and additions.
The Jewish aristocracy, the Romans and the people all have a hand in the affair. Two charges were levelled against Jesus: speaking against the Temple and claiming Messiahship. The latter was not blasphemous, but the Sadducees put a political spin on this when handing Jesus over to Pilate. It meant political agitator. The Passion narratives try to exonerate the Romans in various ways e.g Pilate washing his hands.

- OT influences can be seen in the Passion narratives, especially Psalm 22 and Isaiah 53. The OT recognised the limited atonement brought by the deaths of martyrs; and the sacrificial cult was applied to the death of Christ, as he was seen to fulfil various types of sacrifice. Paul had an original way of interpreting Deuteronomy 21:23. There is no exact parallel to this in the Judaism of the time.
- Hellenistic culture knew of the limited saving significance of the deaths of virtuous kings and men, as well as the scapegoat tradition.

Answering structured and essay questions on Chapter 9

1. **a)** Which way of understanding the cross makes the most sense today?
   b) Which aspects seem to be the most dated and primitive? Can these still carry any spiritual meaning today?
2. Match up the OT reference with the Gospel passages:
   OT: Psalm 22:18; Isaiah 53:12; Psalm 22:1; Psalm 69:21; Psalm 22:7; Proverbs 31:6; Isaiah 53:9.
   NT: Mark 15:26–27; Mark 15:34; Mark 15:24–25; Matthew 27:48–50; Matthew 27:59; Matthew 27:34; Matthew 27:39.
3. Using examples from both Hellenism and Judaism, explain how the early Christians tried to show that the death of Jesus had saving significance.

10 Miracle Stories

KEYWORDS

hagiography – pious legends about a religious figure to idealise them

Hasidim – Jewish holy men who healed the sick

magus – a pagan healer and practitioner of occult skills

miracle – a wonderful event against the laws of nature or working by a higher law

Mishnah – collection of Rabbinical teachings written down by the end of the second century AD

psychosomatic – a physical condition caused by a mental/emotional problem

Talmud – Rabbinic commentaries on the Scriptures, written by the end of the second century AD

1 Introduction

KEY ISSUE Each of the four Gospels presents Jesus as a healer and a performer of **miracles**. Scholars have tried to find parallels to the types of miracle story in Hellenistic and Jewish writings of the time.

Most of the miraculous stories in the Jesus tradition concern healings worked by a combination of touch, spoken word and faith. Several concern raising the dead and a few concern effects upon non-human nature, such as the feeding of the multitude, the cursing of the fig tree, the walking on water and the transition of water into wine. Scholars have tried to find parallels to the types of miracle story in Hellenistic or in Jewish writings of the time. One point of view is that the miraculous was taken for granted in the first century AD and miracle stories were bound to be made up, copied from already existing ones of famous gods and heroes, and added onto the story of Jesus. Others are more cautious, and stress differences between the stories in the Gospels and elsewhere, and suggest that some, at least, might be historical.

This is an account of a pagan healing from Epidaurus:

> A man who could move only one finger of his hand came to the god as a suppliant ... In his sleep he had a vision. It seemed to him that he was playing dice in the room under the temple and was about to throw

> when the god appeared, jumped on his hand and stretched out his fingers ... When day came, he emerged from the sanctuary cured.

There is also the curious tale of the Emperor Vespasian curing a blind man and a man with a paralysed hand. Tacitus reports this in *Histories*, 4, 81. The two men claim that the god Serapis have directed them to ask the Emperor. At first he mocks them and makes light of it, but they beg him. He takes spittle and rubs it on the eyes of the blind man, and touches the other man's hand:

> The hand was instantly restored to use, and the day again shone for the blind man. Both facts are told by eye-witnesses even now when falsehood brings no reward.

(Perhaps these stories demonstrate the power of belief and hope to affect the body – a psychological and **psychosomatic** force that we must still recognise today).

2 Hellenistic miracle stories

People were superstitious in the Hellenistic world and the services of the local **magus** were in demand for cures, blessings and predictions. The classical writer Petronius said, 'the gods walk abroad so commonly in our streets that it is easier to meet a god than a man'. He was mocking the credulity of many of the common people who believed the many characters who claimed to be gods on earth, or who claimed to have magical powers. The healer god Asclepius was immensely popular; the sick filled his temples praying for cures. Apollonius of Tyana was said to have raised a girl from the dead, and to have cured a boy bitten by a dog. The Gospel miracle stories are similar in format to the Hellenistic stories, particularly in Mark. There, Jesus is very much the startling wonder-worker who astounds people by his authority and by his powers over nature (see Mark 1:27–28; 2–12; 4:41; 5:20). There is a petition to be cured or helped, followed by the miraculous event and finally the awe and gratitude of the people.

There are important differences, however:

- The Hellenistic stories are polytheistic. The people pray to many gods, not one
- The magus tried to coax the god into performing a cure by incantations and spells, many examples of which can be seen on surviving Greek papyri from this period. Jesus used no such techniques, relying on the Father's will to heal through him. In Mark 14:32–41 he explicitly relied on the Father's will when in the Garden of Gethsemane. There was no suggestion of using magic to find a supernatural deliverance.

The form of the Gospel stories might have been purposely shaped by the Gospel writers to appeal to a Gentile audience who were used to the magical claims of their magi.

The early Christian writer, Clement of Alexandria could say that Gentiles had no reason to deny the miracle stories of Jesus because their myths were full of them (Stromata vi.3)! Origen argued the same point with the pagan critic, Celsus. The form of the Synoptic miracles does fit that of the Hellenistic tales more closely than Jewish parallels. This does not decide any points of historicity; it simply suggests the genre.

3 Jewish miracle stories

a) The rabbinical writings

The **Talmud** and **Mishnah** contain a few miracle stories. These occur in the context of the belief in the one God of Israel, and some scholars, e.g. Bultmann, feel that these should be taken seriously as parallels for this reason alone. However, Dibelius has shown that the form of the stories is totally different from that in the Gospels. There are two types of rabbinic miracle: those concerning disputes about the Law, and those for the personal enhancement of the teacher. The former usually occur in an argument between two rabbis about the interpretation of a passage in the Torah. One of them performs a miracle to prove his point (which is still not always accepted). The latter are incidental to the teaching of a rabbi, and serve to make him more respected.

b) The Hasidim

A more fruitful source is the series of stories about Galilean holy men who were approached by the local people with requests for prayer. There are the notable cases of Honi the Circle-drawer, who made it rain, and spoke of himself as the son of God. Also Hanina Ben Dosa who was bitten by a snake while praying, and was unaffected; he cured a man's son by prayer and he cured a fever from a distance (compare with the stories and sayings of Jesus in Mark 16:18 and Luke 7:1–10). The Jewish scholar, Geza Vermes, places Jesus among the **Hasidim**, though he admits Jesus is the most outstanding of them. However, Christian scholars do not feel that it is enough to see Jesus as a wandering Galilean holy man, curing the people that came to him. He appears in the Gospels as a man with a mission, the Messiah and herald of God's Kingdom. He is presented as being far more than a preacher or a hermit.

The miracle stories occur early in the Gospel tradition. Peter's sermon in Acts 2:22–24 might contain very early material, and Jesus is presented there as an outstanding miracle worker. Q contains a healing miracle (Matthew 8:5–13); Mark, probably the earliest Gospel, portrays Jesus as a wonder worker. Finally, there is the question of the theology of the miracles in the Gospels. They are not just works of wonder, but signs. They are seen as the dawning of the Kingdom of God, breaking into human history through Jesus. They have an eschatological significance (see, for example, Matthew 11:2–6, where Jesus responds to the Baptist's doubts).

4 Can miracles happen?

a) The Gospels

The Gospels contain numerous miracle stories. Even Q has a healing miracle (the centurion's servant) and the primitive preaching in Acts 2–4 refers to the healing miracles of Jesus. The Jesus tradition always has affirmed that Jesus was a healer and a teacher. It is difficult to cut away the healing stories as later additions, generations later. The handful of nature miracles – walking on water, turning water into wine, feeding the 5,000, calming the storm – are often seen as symbolic stories or exaggerations, but liberal scholars are hard pressed to deny that there is anything behind the healing stories.

The nature miracles can be understood thus:

- Walking on water is a symbol of overcoming evil. The raging waters are a symbol of chaos in the Bible (see Genesis 1:1).
- Turning water into wine is an elaboration of the logia about new wine in new wineskins. Jesus brings the new wine of the new covenant.
- Feeding the 5,000 could be based upon a mutual and spontaneous sharing after the example of Jesus, of openly sharing what little they had.
- Calming the storm could be symbolic of calming emotional turmoils within, or be an exaggeration of Jesus' rebuke to his disciples to stay calm and have faith.

b) The Church

The early Church believed that healing miracles carried on – hence the stories in Acts and the mention of the gift of healing in the Epistles (e.g. 1 Corinthians 12:9, and James 5:14–15). The Church has always believed that healings have carried on – the lives of Celtic monks, Eastern hermits and medieval saints attest to this. Granted that there will be a gloss of legend and **hagiography**, but there is a persistent belief that the risen Lord still heals. This can also be seen in the shrines dotted around Christendom, where cures are recorded – Walsingham in Norfolk, where plaques of thanksgiving are erected by pilgrims, and Lourdes in the South of France, where rigorous tests are applied by a medical team before anyone is declared cured. Modern churches, of all persuasions and styles practise a healing ministry. Catholic, Orthodox and Anglican Churches have the laying on of hands and the anointing of the sick, where blessed oil is applied. Charismatic Christians have the laying on of hands, and some people are recognised as having a ministry of healing. While some extremists have given this a bad name, some of the discredited tele-evangelists in the USA are an example, people do feel genuinely helped by these prayers. Perhaps occurrences of total healing are rare, but many feel an inner strength and peace that helps their overall well-being.

c) Modern science

Scientists are generally sceptical of anything that cannot be measured and predicted. Science observes principles of cause and effect. The supernatural is unpredictable. A closed universe of cause and effect, with regular, immutable laws, has no room for miracles. There are a number of responses to this:

- When a miracle occurs, we might be seeing a higher law at work that we do not understand yet, just as ancient people would have thought an electric light bulb was a miracle a few hundred years ago.
- If 'laws' are only what we normally observe to be happening, then we cannot say that something different might not happen one day.
- We are realising, more and more, that the mind and the body are a unity, how we feel or believe effects how we are. Illness can sometimes be psychosomatic, 'all in the mind', but with a very real effect on the body. Prayers for forgiveness or spiritual healing might affect the body in some cases.
- Even if we accept that there are fixed laws of physics, then it could be argued that the Creator could set these aside to become more directly involved.
- Perhaps we live in a mysterious, vast universe that we are only beginning to understand.

At the end of the day, the historian looking at the Gospel texts can only declare that healing stories were told about Jesus very early on. He or she cannot speak with authority on whether such things can happen or not.

Summary List

- Healings were common in the Hellenistic world, and they are attested in the Gospels in the earliest traditions (e.g. there is one in Q).
- Hellenistic miracles were polytheistic and often involved the skills and spells of a magus.
- Rabbinic miracles were nothing like those of Jesus – they were done to prove a point. Those of the Hasidim were similar e.g. Hanina Ben Dosa and Honi.
- The many healing miracles in the Gospels could be based upon the power of the mind/ faith and psychosomatic illness.

- The small number of nature miracles are sometimes given a symbolic interpretation.
- Healings have been attested throughout Church history, and are still around today.
- Miracles can be explained as the operation of higher laws or the over-ruling of normal laws of cause and effect.

Answering structured and Essay questions on Chapter 10

1. Explain some examples of healings in Hellenistic literature.
2. Read Mark 2:1-11. How might modern science and psychology try to explain this miracle?
3. Examine examples of miracles in Jewish sources and compare these with those of Jesus.
4. 'Miracles don't happen.' How might you answer this statement by using modern scientific ideas and the New Testament material?

11 The Virgin Birth and the Resurrection

KEYWORDS

argument from silence – an assumption, arguing a point when there is no evidence written down

betulah – Hebrew for young woman or virgin, depending on its context

Diaspora – the Jews living outside the Holy Land

Easter faith – the sense of renewed faith and courage within Jesus' disciples

myth – a symbolic story full of coded, spiritual truth

parthenos – Greek for young woman or virgin, depending on its context

1 Introduction

KEY ISSUE The stories of the beginning and the end of Christ's earthly life have been the topic of controversy for some years.

It is a shock for some people to hear that some clergymen do not believe in the literal truth of these stories. A former Bishop of Durham, David Jenkins, made the headlines by his doubts that Jesus was born of a virgin, or that Jesus rose from his body. This section will survey the various issues relating to the text of the NT. This will draw out methods of criticism (exegesis), and questions about the interpretation of the text for the present (hermeneutics).

2 The Virgin Birth

a) The new testament text

The story of Christ's birth from the Virgin Mary appears only in the Gospels of Matthew and Luke (see Matthew 1:18–2:1–12; Luke 2). Mark, probably the earliest Gospel, is silent about the birth of Jesus, beginning with his baptism in the Jordan, by John. The fourth Gospel speaks of the eternal pre-existence of the Logos who was incarnate in the man Jesus; but no details about the actual birth are given. The virgin birth story is not mentioned anywhere else in the New Testament, though Paul alludes to Mary's role in the birth of the Messiah indirectly in Galatians 4:4 '...God sent forth his Son, born of woman...'; John honours the mother of Christ at various places in the Gospel e.g. John 2:1–11 and 19:26–27; and Revelation 12 might allude to Mary and the child Christ. Still, there is no statement that she was a virgin when she conceived. Some see a reference to it in Jesus' lack of a human father in the disputes with the Jews recorded in John 8:19.

While only two books of the New Testament mention the virgin birth, this does not necessarily mean that it did not happen: it might be that it was not of interest for the purposes of the other evangelists, that it was assumed knowledge, or was even kept quiet until later by Mary, for whom it would have been a sensitive issue. Some scholars have felt, though, that its minimal presence in the New Testament suggests it was an imported idea that was not an original part of the Jesus tradition.

b) Isaiah 7:14

Matthew 1:22–23 sees the virgin birth as a fulfilment of Isaiah 7:14 which speaks of a young woman giving birth to a son as a special sign to the people. The Hebrew for 'young woman' is *almah* which usually meant a married woman, but could also mean a virgin (the usual word for virgin was ***betulah***). The Greek LXX used ***parthenos*** which could mean virgin, but could also be taken as a young woman in general (similar in meaning to the old English 'maiden'). Indeed, the only way to tell whether ***parthenos*** means a virgin is to study the context in which it is written.

There is no trace of any expectation of a virgin birth of the Messiah among the Jews at the time of Jesus. Such an idea was alien to them. They obviously did not read Isaiah 7:14 in this light. Matthew is concerned with *pesher* and *midrash* of OT texts to show how the OT was fulfilled in Jesus. He is prepared to be creative in his interpretation, as were the rabbis; and some scholars wonder if he invented the idea of virgin birth by too literal a reading of the verse in Isaiah. (They point out that he is also too literalistic when dealing with Zechariah 9:9, having Jesus riding on an ass and a colt at the same time, when only one is meant in the Hebrew text.) Others suggest that if there was no expectation of a virgin birth for the Messiah in the Judaism of the time, then it is unlikely that Matthew would have read this meaning into the text. Rather, he would have had the tradition of the virgin birth before him, and would have searched through the OT for anything that might suggest it, finding this in Isaiah 7:14.

c) Hellenistic birth stories

Rather than an over-literal reading of Isaiah 7:14, some scholars (e.g. Bultmann) suggest that the virgin birth was imported into the Jesus tradition from the Hellenistic world. The type of myths that Bultmann refers to concern not only the mythical demi-gods, e.g. Heracles, but also the supposed miraculous births of people in history, such as outstanding rulers and philosophers. Alexander the Great had a miraculous birth legend attached to him, even during his lifetime. Plutarch the historian relates some versions of the story, such as that his mother dreamt that a thunderbolt (from Zeus) struck her womb on the night she consummated her marriage, or that a serpent was seen to be sleeping with his mother, and this was a form taken by Zeus-Ammon. Plato is also said to have had a miraculous birth by the union of the god Apollo with his mother. The ancient hero of the Romans, Romulus, had a birth legend ascribed to him, too: Livy the historian states that a vestal virgin was raped and gave birth to twins. It was said that their father was Mars, the god of war. Then again, the philosopher Apollonius was said to be the Egyptian god Proteus, who appeared to his mother in a vision before his birth. These stories were not simple lies, but attempts to stress how special certain people were at the time.

These myths are similar to the Christian virgin birth story, but there are two crucial differences. They are polytheistic, believing that various gods have sired offspring; and the usual way of begetting a divine son is by a god having sexual intercourse with a human woman, often by force or some deception. (In the Greek myths, Zeus disguises himself as a man when he comes to some women.) The NT story is monotheistic, and there is no suggestion that God has sexual intercourse with Mary; a miracle is performed in her womb, as the Lord of creation forms life in her without human intervention. Mary also has freedom to choose whether to bear Jesus or not; it is not forced upon her, or contrived in any way.

Rudolf Bultmann, in his *A Theology of the New Testament*, saw the origin of the virgin birth in:

> ... the mythological conception of a divine son begotten by some deity – an idea which not merely Greek tradition knows, but which is current in the Babylonian and especially the Egyptian king-legend – and was evidently taken over by Jewish Hellenism in Egypt and transferred to the devout men of the Old Testament.
>
> Vol. 1, p. 131

Bultmann assumed that Hellenistic Jews living in the **Diaspora** assimilated these pagan motifs into their religion, and thought of their prophets such as Moses in the same terms. He is overstating his case. Josephus, for example, does present the heroes of the Old Testament in a guise similar to 'divine men', as inspired men full of the Spirit, working wonders and teaching profoundly (Moses is said to be taken to heaven without dying, like Enoch and Elijah) yet they are *not* given miraculous birth legends, or said to be semi-divine.

Such a step was untenable to the Jews. The Old Testament itself has a number of birth legends, e.g. those of Moses and Samuel, as the NT has that of John the Baptist, but these are very different in form. A barren woman cries out to God and she conceives, but by having intercourse with her husband; or the child is miraculously saved from death. Luke is thought to have been a Gentile Christian, and it is just conceivable that he could have Christianised Hellenistic birth stories, but not Matthew, who was a Jewish Christian.

Bultmann felt that there were two competing stories that expressed the divinity of Jesus among the early Christians. There was the miraculous birth story, whereby the child born was the Son of God, and a Spirit-filled wonder worker; and there was the idea of the pre-existent Son who took flesh from Mary (as in Paul, e.g. the hymn in Philippians 2:6–11) and this flowered in the concept of the Logos in John 1:1–18. (Note there is no interest in the details of the birth in John, just that the Logos was incarnate.) These two ideas were joined together later, and the way the Son became incarnate was through a miraculous birth.

Bultmann has noted the different emphases and trends of early Christian confessions, but this does not mean that they were mutually exclusive. There is no reason why the two cannot be held together, and there is no proof that the miraculous birth idea was a later development: we simply cannot say from Paul's silence that he did not know of it. This type of argument is called an **argument from silence**, and is unreliable, because there are too many unknowns.

d) Modern viewpoints

There are puzzles and difficulties with the birth stories in the Gospels, but there is no assured reason for doubting them; many Christians continue to believe them historical. Note the power of the stories in Christian devotion, Christmas festivities, and the mention of the virgin birth in the Church creeds. Others feel that they can be taken as myths, as symbolic stories that put deep spiritual truths and mysteries into story form. So, God was in Jesus in a special and unique way, and the first century way of expressing this was to invent a miraculous birth story. Miracles are difficult to believe in the modern age, and the story does not have to be taken literally to believe that Jesus was 'the Son of God'.

3 The Resurrection

a) The New Testament story

Each of the four Gospels has the story of the empty tomb, and three of the Gospels follow this with stories of appearances of the risen

Jesus. Mark ends abruptly in 16:8, as the women leave the empty tomb, having seen a vision of an angel, and being afraid. The rest of the chapter is a later addition, and some feel that the original ending has been lost. The other Gospels follow this with the risen Jesus appearing, sometimes in a very physical manner, and sometimes in a more mysterious and elusive way (compare Luke 24:36–43; John 20:24–29 with Luke 24:13–31; John 20:11–18, 19–23.) The Jesus who can be touched, who still has the scars from his wounds, appears and disappears mysteriously, even when the doors are locked. Some disciples do not recognise him until he speaks with them, or until he breaks bread. Paul mentions the appearances, but not the empty tomb, in 1 Corinthians 15:3–8. This was written before any of the Gospels, and some think that the empty tomb tradition was a later development added onto the stories of appearances and written into the Gospels. This made the Resurrection sound more dramatic, and more physical, as many ordinary people would have imagined resurrection in this way. The event itself would have been much more spiritual, though, and Paul states that the resurrection body is a mystery, a transformation and a raising into glory that cannot be imagined this side of the grave (see 1 Corinthians 15:35–44). This was in accord with the teaching of some of the Pharisees of the time: resurrection was a raising into glory, and not a resuscitation.

Some of the appearances might have been written to make the resurrection sound more real and tangible, e.g. Luke 24:36–43; the 'doubting Thomas' incident in John 20:24–29 might have been written for the benefit of later believers who had not seen the Lord in the flesh, or even known the apostles (compare the words of the risen Jesus, 'Blessed are those who have not seen and yet believe'). The Emmaus road story might be a reflection on the eucharist, as the early Christians sensed the presence of Jesus with them when they blessed and shared bread and wine.

The appearance to Paul, mentioned in Acts 9, 22 and 26 is more a spiritual presence than a physical encounter, and he does not differentiate between his vision and those of the other apostles earlier (see 1 Corinthians 15:5–8).

The Resurrection in the Epistles is an event that happened to Jesus, but it is experienced as a present reality; it is something existential in the life of the Christian (see Romans 6:4–11; 8:11; 2 Corinthians 3:17f; 4:7–5:15). If the resurrection is compared to a comet passing by, then the place where the comet came from is the event that happened to Jesus at a point in history; the destination is the *parousia* and the coming of the Kingdom; but the present vision of its glowing tail is the experience of new life, grace, freedom from sin, and all the other New Testament metaphors for the Christian life.

However, others point out that the empty tomb story is mentioned in all four of the Gospels, and this should be significant. Paul might allude to it in 1 Corinthians 15:4 (Christ was buried/raised up). He probably took the story for granted, and was not concerned with the emptiness of the tomb in Corinthians, but with the reality of his vision of Christ, to prove that he also had authority as an apostle. The empty tomb story has been believed by Christians through the ages, implied in the creeds, and many feel it should be believed today as there is no convincing reason to question it on the evidence of the New Testament alone. The Resurrection was far more than a physical rising: it was a glorious transformation shared in also by the body of Jesus.

b) Modern views

- Many Christians believe that the tomb was empty and that Jesus was raised up body and soul into glory. They see no strong reason to doubt this from the text of the New Testament.
- Other Christians feel that there are different layers to the traditions, the most primitive of them speaking of appearances and of a spiritual presence. They reject the empty tomb story, but they do believe that Jesus lives on, vindicated by God.
- More radical Christians reject the appearances, feeling that the resurrection event is only to be located in the new life and faith of the disciples (often described as '**Easter faith**').
- Others accept that there might have been visions and various experiences. They stress that faith in the Resurrection need not depend upon these things. It is something personally felt, as an inner renewal. (But some Christians maintain that this bases the Resurrection too much upon human feelings and not upon a fact, an act of God in history.)

c) Old Testament background

Belief in the resurrection of the dead was a late development in the Old Testament. The earliest ideas of an after-life seem to be of a shadowy existence as a ghost in the underworld, called Sheol. Some think there were later ideas of a blessed state in glory (see Psalm 16:10–11) which is not described in any detail. Explicit resurrection ideas are first found in Isaiah 26:19 and Daniel 12:2–4. The latter text is thought to be from the second century BC, from the time of the Maccabees, when many faithful Jews were being martyred rather than worship pagan gods. The Isaiah text is hard to date, but is an early example of apocalyptic. Some see a reference to resurrection in Ezekiel 37 and the breathing of new life into the dry bones. This could have been just a metaphor for the restoration of the nation from the Exile in Babylon. Many Jews did, however, take this as a promise of individual resurrection, as can be seen from excavations at Masada, where scrolls of Ezekiel 37 were found buried where the people lay, having killed themselves before the Romans captured them in the hope of rising again.

It is possible that developing ideas of the covenant led to the belief in resurrection, i.e. the God who made a covenant with his people would still be faithful through death. Persian ideas might have also played their part, with the notion of rewards and punishments for the just and unjust. Popular views of the resurrection were as a physical rising onto a renewed earth, as in 2 Maccabees 7 when a mother loses seven sons, hoping they will return to her in the resurrection.

The apocalyptic writings speak of receiving 'eternal garments' that never wear out (*1 Enoch 62*) and the blessings of the Messianic age which will bring peace and prosperity to the world. (These hopes could bear a more spiritual interpretation as Paul shows in his teaching about the 'spiritual body' in 1 Corinthians 15.) A similar theme was that the resurrection would make people like the angels: Daniel 12 has the blessed 'shining like stars'; *1 Enoch 39:5* says 'the dwelling places of the righteous are with the holy angels'; and the Dead Sea Scrolls speak of a sinful soul being purged and being given a share with 'the holy ones':

> You have made mere humans to share the lots of the spirits of knowledge; to praise your name in their chorus.
>
> 1 QH 3:19–21

(Note also the words of Jesus in Mark 12:25.)

An important theme in the development of the resurrection belief was that of the vindication of righteous martyrs, a strong theme in the Maccabean period. One of the seven sons mentioned above declares to his tormentors:

> you dismiss us from this present life, but the King of the universe will raise us up to an everlasting renewal of life because we have died for his laws.
>
> 2 Maccabees 7:9

The deaths of the martyrs were a partial atonement for the sins of the people, and allowed the great deliverance and victories to take place then. This theme is echoed in the New Testament as Jesus is vindicated by the resurrection, and atones for the sins of the world (compare the early preaching of Peter in Acts 2:22–24, and note also Mark 10:45).

d) Hellenistic background

While the Greeks originally believed in Hades, the shadowy underworld, like Sheol, various beliefs and speculations abounded in the centuries before the birth of Christ. The philosophers, following Plato, believed that the rational soul survived the death of the body. The soul was immortal, but the body was of an inferior, lower order.

The resurrection of the body sounded crude and nonsensical to such Greeks, as in Acts 17:32 when Paul preached in Athens.

Other Greeks believed in reincarnation, where the soul passed into a new body and was reborn with a new identity. The great Pythagoras had held this view.

Still others speculated that the gods would take some mortals to live with them. Stories circulated about the deaths of the divine men: some were taken into heaven, and this taking up of the mortal into the immortal is called apotheosis. Apollonius is said to have entered a temple where he heard maidens singing, 'Hasten thou from earth, hasten thou to heaven, hasten', and his remains were never found. He is also said to have appeared to a doubter after his death and told him to carry on his teaching.

The parallels with the Christian story (and that of the Ascension in Acts 1:9) are obvious, though there are a number of important differences:

- Jesus actually suffered and died, being raised up after this; a Hellenistic divine man would have been taken before his enemies could have executed him.
- Jesus was raised as the exalted Lord over all creation.
- The Resurrection of Jesus inspired his followers to make courageous acts to spread his teaching, making them fearless in the face of death.
- The Christians had (and claim still to have) a sense of a new life, of an inner renewal because Jesus was raised up.
- The story of the Resurrection was handed down (in some form) straightaway, and did not take a dubious length of time to be fabricated and to come to the attention of the literary circles of the day.

e) The Resurrection and history

EP Sanders, in *The Historical Figure of Jesus*, concludes his historical study of the Gospels by considering the resurrection. There are a number of things that can be said, despite the contradictions in the accounts:

- The disciples were disappointed that their hopes of the coming Kingdom were dashed when Jesus died. Yet, something made them start hoping for the Kingdom again. After hiding for a time, they reassembled, and then went on preaching. To quote Sanders:

  That is, *they did not give up his idea that the kingdom would come*; they now expected him to return from heaven to establish it.

  The Historical Figure of Jesus

- The New Testament accounts are clearer about what they deny than what they affirm. They deny that the resurrected Jesus was a ghost or a resuscitated corpse. He was not a phantasm of the night, or a dead body that simply got up again. Jesus was transformed – solid, yet appearing and disappearing at will in the Gospels, and described as spiritual body by Paul (1 Corinthians 15). Comparing Paul and Luke, Sanders says:

> Both authors were trying to describe – Paul at first hand, Luke at second or third hand – an experience that does not fit a known category ... Faced with accounts of this nature – sharply diverging stories of where and to whom Jesus appeared, lack of agreement and clarity on what he was like (except agreement on negatives) – we cannot reconstruct what really happened.
>
> *The Historical Figure of Jesus*

- The disciples all agreed that Jesus was raised, but they could not agree upon the exact sequence of events, or who had seen him. These men were prepared to die for their cause – it does not seem to have been a deliberate scam.

> Moreover, a calculated deception should have produced greater unanimity. Instead there seem to have been *competitors*: 'I saw him first!' 'No! I did'. The very untidiness of the accounts might suggest that something really was going on.
>
> *The Historical Figure of Jesus*

- Paul did not distinguish between his visionary experience and that of the other disciples. Yet he asserts that Jesus was in a 'spiritual body'. He, also, at first hand, wants to deny that Jesus was a mere spirit or ghost.

In conclusion, Sanders states:

> That Jesus' followers (and later Paul) had resurrection experiences is, in my judgement, a fact. What the reality was that gave rise to the experiences I do not know ... we know that after his death his followers experienced what they described as the 'resurrection': the appearance of a living but transformed person who had actually died. They believed this, they lived it, and they died for it. In the process they created a movement, a movement that in many ways went far beyond Jesus' message. Their movement grew and grew ...
>
> *The Historical Figure of Jesus*

Historians can only describe the fact that something happened to the disciples, that they claimed 'resurrection appearances', just as historians can only claim that the first Christians believed Jesus had worked miracles. They are not competent to judge whether such spiritual, supernatural things can happen. In a way, such events are outside history as they are not to be found in the normal chain of physical cause and effect. That something happened to real people in history cannot be doubted, though.

Summary List

The Resurrection appearances:

- Matthew – In Jerusalem, to the two Marys, and then in Galilee, to the Eleven.
- Mark – An angel appears to the two Marys and Salome in Jerusalem. It is promised that Jesus will appear to them and the Eleven in Galilee.
- Luke – The angel appears to the women in Jerusalem, promising an appearance in Galilee. Jesus appears to two disciples on the road to Emmaus. Jesus appears to the Eleven in Jerusalem, later that day.
- John – Jesus appears to Mary Magdalene in Jerusalem, and then to the Eleven over a period of forty days. He appears to seven disciples in Galilee.
- I Corinthians – Jesus appears to Cephas (Peter), then the Twelve, then 500 disciples at once, then James, then finally, Paul.

Difficulties with the virgin birth story:

- Only two of the Gospels mention it. The rest of the New Testament is silent.
- Mark, the earliest Gospel, does not mention anything special about Christ's birth, nor does the *kerygma*, i.e. the preaching of the apostles.
- Isaiah 7:14 does not necessarily mean a virgin, but simply a young woman.
- There was no expectation that the Messiah would be born of a virgin in first-century Judaism.

But

- The story is mentioned in two Gospels, but with different details and stories. That there was a virgin birth is consistent to both accounts.
- Isaiah 7:14 *could* be interpreted as a virgin.
- If there was no expectation of a virgin birth among the Jews, why has Matthew read this into Isaiah 7:14? Perhaps he has the tradition, and reworks an old text to fit it. The virgin birth might not have been expected, but it might have happened as a surprising act of God.

Thinking about the Resurrection:

- Resurrection belief developed slowly in the OT, based on the covenant and God's commitment to his people. This flourished in apocalyptic texts by the time of Jesus.
- The Hellenistic equivalent is the apotheosis of a virtuous man.
- All four Gospels contain the story of the empty tomb, but other NT writings stress that the Resurrection is a spiritual presence or an inner illumination.
- Modern scholars hold different views:
  – the Resurrection was an interior affair in the disciples
  – the Resurrection involved visions and experiences
  – the Resurrection involved the above and also the empty tomb.

- There is an irreducible 'X' factor about the Resurrection – something changed the scared disciples.
- Sanders comments on the honest testimonies that are rough and ready and have not been smoothed out.

Answering structured and essay questions on Chapter 11

1. What hope of an after-life can be found in the OT?
2. Why does Jesus appeal to Torah passages in his debate with the Sadducees? (Mark 12:25)
3. Why does Sanders think there is a historical basis for the resurrection?
4. List the arguments for and against the historicity of the virgin birth.

12 Who is Jesus?

KEYWORDS

Christology – study of Christ

embryonic Christology – a primitive understanding of Christ, pregnant with possibilities for future development

hypostasis – a projection of part of God into creation

Kyrios – Lord

Logos – Greek for 'Word'/'Reason' – a hypostasis of God

Messiah – God's anointed one, the coming King

Son of God – the Messiah, a righteous man or man filled with God

Son of Man – 'oneself', and a title for a future deliverer based on Daniel 7:13

Sophia – 'Wisdom' – a hypostasis of God in creation

1 Introduction

KEY ISSUE There are differences in the way Jesus is presented in the New Testament, and there are various titles used of him, e.g. Teacher, Messiah/Christ, Lord, **Son of God**, **Son of Man**, and the Word (**Logos**). The fact that Jesus attracted so many diverse titles from the Old Testament, the Judaism of his time, and even the Hellenistic world, shows how singular and outstanding he was to the Christians.

It is debated how many of these titles, if any, Jesus himself used. Some might have come from the first Christians, to confess their faith in Jesus. The impetus for all this was the belief that the salvation of God, the Kingdom itself, had come in this man from Nazareth. Christians felt saved through him. They felt themselves to be in a new relationship with God, whom they called 'Abba, Father', as did Jesus (Mark 14:36 compared with Romans 8:15–16).

The resurrection was the real starting point for **Christology** (study of Christ). The Resurrection put all that Jesus had said and done in a new light. Who was this man that something so dynamic should happen to him? Traces of an **embryonic Christology** can be seen in

Peter's speech in Acts 2:36, and in Romans 1:3. Here Jesus is made **Messiah** at the Resurrection. Or is it simply that he was *declared* to be the Messiah at that point, but had been so all along?

The Synoptic Gospels present a different portrait of Jesus from that of the fourth Gospel. In the Synoptics, Jesus appears to be a human being, filled with the Spirit, and working miracles by the power of God, but in John he is more like a god, the Word of God incarnate. While in Mark 6:5 Jesus could not perform any cures because the people there did not have faith in him, the Jesus in John seems to be able to do what he wants, whenever he wants. Also, in the Synoptics, Jesus has a limited knowledge: he does not know when the Kingdom will come in Mark 13:3, but in John, he knows everything, including what people are thinking (see John 13:3; 2:24–25). Charles Talbert, in *What is a Gospel?*, shows how the Synoptics follow the myth of the immortals: the idea of an inspired man who did great deeds, and was then taken up to heaven. The fourth Gospel follows a 'descending/ascending' myth, of a deity who becomes a man, does great deeds, and then returns to the heavenly realm. (Note the frequency in John of the theme of the Son being sent by the Father and returning to him.) While a clear development can be seen from the Christology of the Synoptics to that of John, the former still speak of Jesus in outstanding, remarkable terms. Jesus speaks with authority, unlike other teachers (Mark 1:27–28) and feels able to set aside aspects of the Torah, in his own name (see Matthew 5:21–22), something that no other rabbi would have dared to do. His miracles are seen as signs of the Kingdom of God dawning (see Matthew 11:2–6) and not just answers to prayer, as with the Galilean Hasidim. There is a strong and high Christology here, however ill-defined, which sees Jesus as more than a prophet.

The epistles, written before the Synoptics, contain a higher Christology that is more akin to that in John. In Philippians 2:5–11 there is a hymn that celebrates the descending/ascending redeemer, who is given the 'name above every name' after his resurrection (i.e. '**Kyrios**', Lord, a divine title). This hymn was probably quoted by Paul, and predated his epistle, placing this belief back into the forties or fifties AD. A similar hymn is found in Colossians 1:15–20 where Christ is called 'the first-born of all creation', referring to his chief status over all other things. Christ is given a similar cosmic dimension in Ephesians 1:20–23, and Paul uses the descending/ascending motif in 2 Corinthians 8:9, clearly teaching that there was an incarnation.

The Synoptics seem to preserve a very early view of Christ, taken from the traditions of his deeds and words, but the Epistles show how he was understood after his Resurrection, in the life and faith of the early Church. It is but a short step from there to the Jesus of John.

2 The Messiah

KEY ISSUE The word 'Messiah' means 'anointed one' in Hebrew. 'Christ' is the Greek equivalent. 'Jesus Christ' therefore means 'Jesus the Christ'. As a Jewish title it is therefore one of the most primitive titles of Jesus.

The Jews hoped for various types of Messiah. There were three basic models: that of a king Messiah, a High Priest Messiah, and a prophet Messiah.

a) The King Messiah

This idea was based upon the practice of anointing the Jewish kings at their coronation. Each Old Testament king had been a Messiah. 2 Samuel 7:14 was seen as a Messianic text, where David was promised that a son of his would establish his kingdom and reign forever. The original meaning of this was that God blessed David's reign and dynasty, and the son referred to Solomon who built the Temple. Yet, the kingdom had been lost, and was now in the hands of the Romans and their puppet kings. The king Messiah, 'the Son of David' would be a great warrior, restoring the Golden Age under David. He would be holy, and his righteousness would also attract the Gentiles, as is shown in this apocalyptic passage from the mid first century BC.

> See, Lord, raise up for them their king, the son of David,
> In the time which thou knowest, O God,
> To reign over Israel thy servant;
> and gird him with strength to shatter the unjust rulers ...
> He will possess the nations, to serve beneath his yoke;
> He will glorify the Lord with the praise of all the earth.
> He will cleanse Jerusalem in holiness, as it was of old,
> That the nations may come from the ends of the earth to see his glory,
> Bearing as gifts her sons who had fainted,
> And to see the glory of the Lord with which God has glorified her
> A righteous king, taught by God, is their ruler,
> And there will be no unrighteousness among them all his days,
> For all will be holy, and their king the Anointed Lord.'

Psalms of Solomon 17:23f, 32–6

This was also the main hope at Qumran, as they prepared for the final battle against the Romans and the coming of the New Age. At this point, the king Messiah merged with apocalyptic hopes of a renewed earth, and some Persian influence might have made some think of him as a more supernatural figure (see Section 5). Still, the main idea was of a human warrior who would restore the nation and bring peace.

b) The High Priest Messiah

This figure is mentioned in an inter-testamental work, the *Testament of Levi 18*. He was expected at Qumran, as seen in the *Community Rule*: 'until there shall come the Prophet and the Messiahs of Aaron and Israel'. They expected two Messiahs, a King and High Priest after the close liaison between Moses and Aaron the priest, and between Zerubbabel and the high priest Joshua, after the Exile (see Zechariah 3–4). In the second Jewish revolt (AD 132–5) Bar Cochba worked with the priest, Eleazar.

c) The Prophet Messiah

This figure was identified with the prophet mentioned in Deuteronomy 18:15–18. The text states that God will raise up a prophet like Moses to guide them after his death. It is no more than a promise that the prophetic ministry will continue; but the rabbis saw Moses as head and shoulders above all the other prophets and therefore another prophet like him would be special. Thus the verse became Messianic. The prophet is mentioned briefly at Qumran (see above quotation) and was possibly identified with their founder, the Teacher of Righteousness. This prophet is also mentioned in the questions put to John the Baptist (John 1:21). There was also the associated tradition of the return of Elijah as the herald of the Kingdom/Messiah, because in the Old Testament he was taken to heaven without dying.

d) Jesus as the Messiah?

- At the time of Jesus, there were varieties of Messianic expectation, with some figures heralding the new age, and some initiating it. Central issues were the restoration of the kingdom of Israel and liberation from Roman rule. The idea of a Messiah crucified and killed by the Romans was a nonsense to the Jews (note 1 Corinthians 1:23).
- We have seen how the earliest thinking of the Church might have been to declare that Jesus was made the Messiah at the Resurrection; they expected him to return in glory and transform the earth. The birth-pangs of the Kingdom of God were upon them. The Gospels present the idea of a suffering Messiah, who brings the dawning of the Kingdom in his person, but who must suffer before the new age will fully come. This draws upon the motif of the Suffering Servant in Isaiah 53, and the idea of a suffering Son of Man suggested in Daniel 7:25.

- Whether Jesus himself ever claimed to be the Messiah is a moot point. The early Church certainly claimed that he was, and it was one of the first titles he was hailed with after the Resurrection. The Gospels show Jesus as being wary of the title: he cautions people to remain silent when they call him Messiah (e.g. Mark 1:40–44; 8:29–30). Even at his trial, when the High Priest asked him directly, he replied, 'You have said so' according to Matthew 26:64 (though Mark 14:62 has him saying, 'I am'). The title most used by Jesus in the Gospels is the Son of Man, not the Messiah.
- Wrede, in 1901, argued that Mark had joined together various stories about Jesus with the theme of the Messianic secret, the idea that Jesus was keeping his identity hidden until his trial and crucifixion. This was a creation of the evangelist, to explain why Jesus had not openly claimed to be the Messiah. Bultmann also thought that Jesus had never identified himself with the Messiah. This is possible, but it could be argued that Jesus was wary about using the title because of its political overtones: it would invite trouble from the Romans, and detract from his idea of bringing a more spiritual Kingdom into the hearts of believers as a precursor to the dawning of the new age (see the writings of T W Manson and F F Bruce).
- John Miller, in *Jesus at Thirty*, examines the Temptation narratives from a psychological perspective. He sees a consistent rejection of power in the teaching and ministry of Jesus:

> ...the actual content of these temptations is similar. All three seek to entice Jesus into fantasizing extraordinary feats of the most grandiose nature (turn stones into bread, fall safely from a great height, rule the world). But what in substance is Satan actually confronting Jesus with in these seemingly bizarre suggestions? It is difficult not to see in the background here messianic fantasies of one sort or another, for to work mighty signs and to rule the world were the then prevailing expectations of what a miracle working Messiah would do when he appeared ... In summary then, it is not, as traditionally thought, the Messiah who is here being tempted, but Jesus, fresh from an experience of repentance, forgiveness, and 'sonship', who is tempted by messianism.
>
> *Jesus at Thirty*, pp. 59–60

3 The Logos

KEY ISSUE John 1:1–18 is a hymn to the Logos (Greek: 'the Word') who became incarnate in Jesus of Nazareth.

The Word is mentioned in the Old Testament alongside the Spirit, as the power and presence of God in action in the world ('God acting towards us' – John Hick). In Genesis 1 God speaks words which bring Creation into being, and the Spirit renews the creation (see Psalm 104:30). The Hebrew *dabar* (word) suggested the power of the person who spoke it, and not just the abstract idea. We might speak of empty words, but an ancient would think of binding oaths and solemn pronouncements. Philo, a Jewish thinker from Egypt at the time of Jesus, speculated about the Logos as the agent of Creation, being the immanent power of the transcendent, invisible God. Indeed, he said, people are made in the image of the Logos, and participate in him by reason. People are the sons of God because they are in the image of the Logos, who is the primal Son of God. Much of what Philo said is similar to John, and to the Christian idea of being 'in Christ' and adopted as sons of God through him; but Philo never suggests that the Logos became incarnate in history. This is a novel idea.

The Greeks also used the idea of the Logos in their philosophy as the reason immanent in the universe that bound it together in cosmic harmony.

A similar idea can be seen in the Wisdom of God, treated poetically in Proverbs 8 as an aspect of his being and as an expression of his power. This is developed under Hellenistic influence in the apocryphal book, the Wisdom of Solomon 7, and sounds like the Greek Logos, 'pervading and penetrating all things by her pureness ... the breath of the power of God... a clear effluence of the glory of the almighty'. Christ was thought of in these terms in Hebrews 1:3, and is incarnate Wisdom in 1 Corinthians 1:24. The Jews were prepared to speak of the hypostases (aspects/extensions) of God who acted in the world, but they were not incarnate. Christian belief in the incarnation of Wisdom/the Logos led to envisaging the divine hypostases as personal, and this laid the foundations for the doctrine of the Trinity, that there were three persons in the one God.

4 Son of God

KEY ISSUE This is perhaps the most common title for Jesus amongst Christians, but it is used as a description of Jesus by people other than himself in the Gospels, whether angels, Roman centurions, demons or disciples.

There are only two sayings where Jesus refers to himself as 'the Son', in Mark 13:32 and Matthew 11:27. Jesus does not explicitly call himself 'Son of God', though. 'The Son' might be short for 'Son of Man', the title usually placed upon his lips in the Gospels. C K Barrett feels that Jesus' divine sonship played no part in his original teaching, but has been written into the Gospels later. The origin and meaning of this title are therefore not as straightforward as many would think.

a) Old Testament background

(i) The faithful Israelite

Hosea 11:1 describes Israel as God's son: 'Out of Egypt I called my son'. This sense is carried through into the Apocrypha, as in Ecclesiasticus and the Wisdom of Solomon. Ben Sira wrote: 'Be a father to the fatherless, and as a husband to widows, and God shall call you son.' The author of Wisdom said: 'the just man is God's son'.

(ii) The King

Psalm 2 is a coronation psalm for the Israelite King. He is hailed as God's son because he is to be anointed with God's Spirit to give faithful counsel to the people. He is to be a faithful servant and shepherd of the nation : 'You are my son, today I have begotten you' (Psalm 2:7). 2 Samuel 7:14 presents a promise to King David, through the lips of the prophet Nathan, that his dynasty would be blessed by God and would reign forever : 'I will be his father, and he shall be my son'.

(iii) The Messiah

There is no clear or widespread evidence of 'Son of God' being used as a Messianic title outside the New Testament. A fragment of the Dead Sea Scrolls, however, links Psalm 2:7 with 2 Samuel 7:14 and is given a Messianic interpretation.

(iv) The Hasidim

These Jewish holy men of the second century BC, such as Hanina and Honi, were known as God's sons (as were all just Jews of the time); their miracles of healing and rain-making were thought to stem from their closeness to God. They called God 'Father' rather than the usual, and formal, 'Lord of the universe' then current. Hanan, the grandson of Honi, called God 'Abba' in prayer, a word that suggested a tender closeness, and was used by Palestinian children to their fathers. Some people came to Hanan calling him 'Abba' and asking him to pray for rain. His prayer went:

> Lord of the universe, render a service to those who cannot distinguish between the Abba who gives rain and the Abba who does not.

'Abba' was the special way that Jesus had of addressing God in prayer. Jeremias claimed that this was a unique usage and showed that Jesus had a special awareness of God as his Father. He overstated his case, as Vermes has shown by pointing to the Hasidic use of 'Abba' just mentioned; but Jesus is distinctive in the frequency that he calls God 'Father', whether using the term 'Abba' or a similar word (e.g. Mark 14:36, Matthew 6:9).

b) The early Church

Psalm 2:7 and 2 Samuel 7:14 were linked together and used Messianically. This lies behind Romans 1:3 where Jesus is declared Son of God at the resurrection, and is implied in Peter's speech in Acts 2 where Jesus is greater than David as the risen Lord and Messiah. The voice at the baptism links Psalm 2:7 with Isaiah 42:1, linking the Son of God and the Servant together (see Mark 1:11 and parallels). It is impossible to know whether Jesus ever called himself 'Son of God'; he might have done, at least in the sense of being the Messiah. Note that Matthew 11:27 is a very early saying, from Q, and likely to be an authentic logion of Jesus.

It is also possible that Jesus called himself 'Son of God' and was called this by others, as the Jewish Hasidim were. (The centurion's confession probably read 'Truly, this man was a son of god', meaning a Hellenistic divine man.) The Resurrection produced a rethinking, and Jesus was recognised as the promised Messiah/Son of God, and the title was written back into the Gospel tradition. Jesus' teaching authority and his distinctive sense of sonship, using 'Abba' so frequently, and the sense of the Kingdom breaking in through his miracles, would have been fruitful material for reflection. The Resurrection speeded up the process.

c) Hellenism

Augustus and subsequent emperors were given the title 'son of god' or 'son of Zeus'. It could suggest a strong ruler who brought peace and unity; a wise philosopher; a miracle worker; or a demigod, resulting from the union between a god and a mortal. The title 'Son of God' might have been used so widely by the early Church because it could appeal to Gentiles as well as to Jews, although it took on a different meaning for Gentiles, not simply the Messiah, but an outstanding divine-human figure who brought salvation. In Acts 9:20, Paul's message is simply, 'Jesus is the Son of God' and in 1 Thessalonians 1:10 the Son is like a divine being alongside the living God who would soon appear from heaven to bring the world to an end. Mark depicts Jesus as a wonder worker and exorcist. However, the Christian 'Son' was unique, and not just one among many.

Rudolf Bultmann's Theology of the New Testament adds:

> Hellenistic-Jewish Christians had brought along the title 'Son of God' embedded in their missionary message; for the earliest Church had

> already called Jesus so. But one must recognise that the title, which originally denoted the messianic king, now takes on a new meaning which was self-evident to Gentile hearers. Now it comes to mean the divinity of Christ, his divine nature, by virtue of which he is differentiated from the human sphere; it makes the claim that Christ is of divine origin and is filled with divine 'power'... That the proclamation of 'Christ, the Son of God', was so understood, is not to be wondered at; the figure of a Son of God was familiar to Hellenistic ways of thinking, familiar in several variations ... The Hellenistic period knows a whole series of such 'divine men' (*theioi andres*), who claimed to be sons of [a] god or were regarded as such, and some of whom were also cultically worshipped.
>
> *A Theology of the New Testament*, pp. 128–30

5 Son of God to God the Son

Saying that 'Son of God' meant the Messiah was one thing, but it was another story to claim Jesus as a divine being, as can be seen in the Epistles (e.g. 1 Thessalonians 1:10; Philippians 2:5–11 and Colossians 1:15–20) and so confidently in John. 'Son of God' possibly took on divine implications once it moved out into the Hellenistic world. The final stage was in the formation of the creeds, when the Son is co-equal with the Father and the Spirit from all eternity, and here this means not Jesus the man but the God who was incarnate in him and was the subject of his experiences.

For some, this was an illegitimate step. The writers in *The Myth of God Incarnate* (Don Cupitt and John Hick), also saw this as so much fabrication, a piece of poetic mythology stressing how special and precious Jesus was.

On the other hand, the development of the tradition can be seen as drawing out the implications of what was originally there. The special authority of Jesus, his miracles, and his Resurrection made people see him as far more than human. The early Gospel material speaking of the Son of Man, the Messiah and the inspired exorcist/healer presented only an embryonic portrait, a Christology pregnant with meaning that the Church developed under the guidance of the Holy Spirit. Such are the views of more traditional scholars such as C F D Moule, in *The Origin of Christology*. Martin Hengel in *The Son of God* argues that Jesus came to be seen as a divine figure because God's salvation was so final in him; whereas other teachers and prophets gave only partial insights into God, or had a limited saving effect, the death and Resurrection of Jesus were seen to have cosmic implications (see Hebrews 1:1–2; Romans 8:19–20).

6 Son of Man

a) In the Old Testament

The phrase, 'son of man' is used in Psalm 8:4 and Ezekiel 2:1 for a human being, a mortal. In Daniel 7:13 there is 'one like a son of man' described in an apocalyptic passage. This figure comes on the clouds from the Ancient of Days as the Kingdom is delivered to the saints of God. The figure represents the faithful Israelites who were undergoing persecution by Antiochus Epiphanes when this was written; he is a corporate figure, like the Servant in Isaiah 53, representing the people. 'Son of man' would therefore seem to mean 'a man', a human being', according to the Old Testament:

> I saw one like a son of man coming with the clouds of heaven. And he came to the Ancient One and was presented before him. To him was given dominion and glory and kingship, that all peoples, nations and languages should serve him.
>
> Daniel 7:13–14

b) In the New Testament

In the New Testament it is used as a title of Jesus, carrying the definite article, 'the Son of Man'. It is only ever spoken in the Gospels by Jesus, and never by his disciples. It is used 69 times in the Synoptics, and 13 times in John. It is used only once in the rest of the New Testament, in Acts 7:56, when Stephen sees the ascended Lord before his death, and this is the only occasion of the title being used by a disciple for his Lord. Sometimes Jesus uses it to speak about himself generally (Matthew 8:20), or about his passion (Mark 9:31, 10:45), and eschatologically (Mark 8:38).

The eschatological use suggests a reliance upon Daniel 7:13. The problem is that there is no known use in Jewish literature between the two testaments of the title 'the Son of Man' as a heavenly redeemer figure, or as a title of the Messiah. Its popularity in the Gospels, and its almost complete absence in the rest of the New Testament is therefore a puzzle.

c) Other apocalyptic writings

The use of the title is attested in the *Book of Enoch*, and 2 Esdras. 2 Esdras is post-NT, but *Enoch* has been found at Qumran, except the crucial section containing the title, 37–71, known as the 'Similitudes'. It is therefore possible that the New Testament influenced this section which was added later; it is unlikely to have been by a

Christian hand as Enoch is called the Son of Man, but Christian usage could have influenced some Jewish thinking.

d) An early Christian confession?

Some scholars believe that the use of the title Son of Man for Jesus originated with the earliest Christian communities. Lohmeyer sees its origin with the Galilean Christians, and Cullmann with the Hellenists (see Acts 6). If so, it is surprising to find the title *only* on the lips of Jesus in the Gospels. Others have traced its origin to Paul's statements about the first man, Adam, and Jesus as the second Adam (1 Corinthians 15:45).

e) The Son of Man and the Kingdom

Some logia of Jesus in the Synoptics can be compared and set in parallel. Here, one has 'Son of Man' where the other has 'the Kingdom of God' (compare Matthew 16:28 with Luke 9:27, Mark 9:1). The proclamation of the Kingdom of God is widely agreed to be a genuine Jesus tradition; the overlapping of the Son of Man is intriguing.

f) A manner of speech

Recent research into the title has suggested that it was an Aramaic idiom, referring to oneself; 'son of man': a person, i.e. the speaker, 'one', 'I'. There is a good deal of debate about whether the 'son of man' form was so used in Aramaic in the first century AD, but the Jewish scholar, Vermes, argues that it was, as well as a similar form, 'this man'. He quotes various examples, and points out that it was a polite, tactful manner of speech that was meant to be ambiguous. Its use would often be followed by a clear assertion of who it referred to, as in Mark 2:10: 'To convince you that the son of man has the right on earth to forgive sins ... I say to you ...'

Some of the parallel logia of Jesus in the Synoptics show that the 'son of man' phrase appeared as 'I' in other versions. So, Matthew 16:13 says 'Who do men say that the Son of man is?' but this becomes 'Who do men say that I am?' in Mark 8:27 (compare Matthew 5:11 and Luke 6:22; Matthew 10:32 and Luke 12:8).

g) A future person?

Some scholars, such as Bultmann, have wondered whether Jesus was speaking about someone who was to come after him, when speaking of the Son of Man. They point out that Mark 8:38 sounds as though Jesus is referring to someone else, a future deliverer. After his

Resurrection, the early Church might have identified Jesus with this figure, i.e. Jesus was the one who would come in glory. This view has not gained widespread acceptance. Vermes in *Jesus and the World of Palestinian Judaism,* pp. 89–99 has a penetrating critique of Bultmann's view of the Son of Man as a future person, other than Jesus. Vermes writes from a Jewish perspective, using knowledge of Aramaic literature and inscriptions, noting similar terms such as 'hahu gabra' (that man) and how they are used indirectly for the speaker e.g. 'Does "hahu gabra" want a burial place? Give *me* the money and keep the burial place for yourself!'.

h) A deliberately vague title?

F F Bruce argues that Jesus deliberately chose to use the Son of Man title because it was not in vogue in the Judaism of his time. It was an apocalyptic description of a redeemer figure that he could easily apply to himself. The advantage of using a new title, and a neglected Old Testament passage, meant that he could fill this with his own meaning. The title 'Messiah' was a politically loaded term that he wanted to avoid, and hence the theme of the Messianic secret in Mark, whereas Jesus calls himself the Son of Man quite openly.

i) Conclusions

- Some could maintain that Jesus did not call himself 'Son of Man', but that this was the confession of the first Christians after his Resurrection, when they recognised him as the figure in Daniel 7:13.
- Recent scholarship suggests that Jesus used the 'son of man' phrase as a self-description in the idiom of his time. Later Christians then linked this with Daniel 7:13, reworking his 'son of man' logia as conveying a Messianic, divine rule.
- Still others feel that Jesus himself understood his mission in the light of Daniel 7:13, cleverly linking this figure with the Suffering Servant in Isaiah 53.
- Lindars questions such a direct use of the text by Jesus, but feels that Jesus' vague self-references were combined with a sense of being the unique agent of the coming of God's Kingdom. It was then easy for the early Church to apply Daniel 7:13 to Jesus.

Summary List

- The Resurrection was the real starting point for Christology (the study of the person of Christ). Whatever Jesus said about himself, it was who he was after the Resurrection that mattered.
- The Synoptic portraits of Christ are different from the fourth Gospel – an inspired, empowered man who does not know everything/an incarnate God who knows what people are thinking, and remembers living in heaven before he became man.

- The Synoptics follow the Greek idea of an inspired man who was taken into heaven. The Fourth Gospel has the descending/ascending myth of a deity who becomes mortal and then returns.
- The Epistles, written before the Synoptics, reveal a higher Christology – the descending/ascending myth, and divine titles are used of Christ.
- There is an implicit Christology in the Synoptics whereby Christ is uniquely empowered by God's Spirit, and has a special authority.
- There were different conceptions of the Messiah (King/High Priest/Prophet) and Jesus was ambivalent about using the title. Was this to avoid political associations and unwanted confrontation?
- 'Son of God' can be understood on different levels and did not mean a divine being within the pages of the NT. It was a righteous, inspired man, specially filled by God, and the chosen King.
- 'Son of Man' is an original Christological title, unparalleled in the OT or the Judaism of the first century. It is based on the vision of Daniel, and might be reflexive – 'I', 'myself.'
- The Logos had been adopted by Judaism as a divine **hypostasis**, working within the creation, but the NT concept of the Logos taking flesh was unknown and unparalled.

Answering structured and essay questions on Chapter 12

a) Planning an essay

The material below is to help you prepare an essay on 'The Son of Man as a Christological title'.

a) The title as used in Judaism before, and at the time of, the life of Jesus:
- Daniel 7:13–14
- *I Enoch* ('Similitudes' pre- or post-Christian?)

b) The title as used in the NT
- Summarise its use in the Gospels and in Acts 7:56
- Compare the 'Son of Man' and 'Kingdom of God' sayings.

c) The title used by Jesus?
- As a future person?
- As a turn of phrase for 'one', 'I'?
- As a deliberately vague title?

d) The title as the first Christian confession?
- Post-Easter confession?
- Later reflection and the link with the Passion story and Isaiah 53?
- Filling out the vague self-references of Jesus?
- Filling out vague hopes of vindication and glory that Jesus had?

b) Questions

1. Read Matthew 11:27. What might Jesus have meant by 'Son' here? Why is this language strange in the Synoptics?
2. Read Mark 15:39. What would the centurion have actually said, and what would he have meant by this?
3. Read Matthew 26:63–64. What does the High priest call Jesus, and how does Jesus respond (compare with the scene in Luke 22:67–71)
4. Describe how 'Son of God' is used in the following passages, noting any OT ideas: Luke 1:35; Matthew 3:13–17; Mark 1:9–11; Luke 3:21–22; Matthew 17:1–9; Mark 9:2–10; Luke 9:28–36.
5. Eduard Schweitzer in ***Jesus, the Parable of God*** suggests that the sayings and parables of the Synoptics have a Christology all of their own before special titles and concepts were used of Christ. He is the one through whom God's kingdom and blessing comes. He is a shepherd searching for the lost, or a father welcoming a lost son. Look at these parables and see what role Jesus identifies himself with in them: Luke 15:4 7, 8 10; Mark 4:13–20.
6. Read the Temptation narrative in Matthew 4:1–11. List the three temptations, and explain how these are temptations to be a certain type of Messiah. Which model of Messiah does this fit most closely – King Messiah, High Priest Messiah or Prophet Messiah?
7. What leads some people to suggest that Jesus was first recognised as the Messiah after his Resurrection?
8. The following characteristics are true of 'divine men' in Hellenistic belief:
   - **Miraculous birth from a human woman by a god's power**
   - **A god walked the earth, disguised as a human being**
   - **Supernatural powers, usually of healing**
   - **Great wisdom and insight, perhaps prophesying the future**
   - **Great strength and prowess in battle.**

a) Compare these Gospel passages about Jesus with the ideas of 'divine men': Mark 4:35–41; Luke 1:30–35; Mark 13:28–31; Jn 20:26–28; Mark 1:40–45.

b) There are important differences between Jesus and 'divine men'. Compare the following passages: Mark 10:45; Mark 15:39; Luke 23:34.

9. Whichever titles Jesus used of himself, the first Christians ascribed to him all the titles that were available to them for redeemer figures, and of the power and action of God in their midst. This process began very early.

a) List the meanings of 'Logos' in the OT and in Greek thought.

b) How does the NT identify Jesus with the Logos?

10. From C F D Moule's The Origin of Christology (p. 2):

> **one might say that it starts with a Palestinian Rabbi and ends with the divine lord of a Hellenistic Saviour cult, and that it explains the transition from the one to the other in much the same way as popular**

> science may exhibit... the evolution of *homo sapiens* from lemur or ape in a diagrammatic tree, marking the emergence of each new species and assigning successive periods to them … I find my own reading of the evidence leading me to the view that development is a better analogy for the genesis of Christology than evolution... development... will mean something more like the growth, from immaturity to maturity, of a single specimen from within itself.

How does he explain the different ideas of Christ in the NT, and the various meanings of 'Son of God'?

13 Did Jesus Intend to Found the Church?

KEYWORDS

adoptionism – belief that Jesus became the Christ and Son of God at his baptism

apostate – someone who abandons the faith

Ebionites – literally 'poor ones' – a later Jewish Christian sect which followed the Law, held an adoptionist view of Jesus, and saw Paul as an apostate

ekklesia – Greek for 'assembly', and the NT term for 'church'

grace – unmerited favour ; the forgiving love of God in action

Judaisers – Jewish Christians who tried to force Gentile converts to follow the Law

justification by faith – to be made acceptable to God by an inner transformation, by trusting in Christ's cross.

Nazarenes – another later Jewish Christian sect

parousia – return of Christ

1 Introduction

KEY ISSUE Jesus, in the Synoptics, proclaims the imminent arrival of the Kingdom of God. He points beyond himself, though he is proclaimer and messenger. In the New Testament, post-Easter, Jesus is proclaimed by the Church. Did Jesus ever envisage that his followers would go on after him, and found a community?

'Church' is from the Greek, ***ekklesia***, 'assembly'. The Jesus movement was called by various terms before the term Church was established – the Way, the Nazarenes, Christians. The Synoptic tradition has logia about the church in Mt 18:15–22. These might have been placed upon the lips of Jesus post-Easter. An original logion might be in 18:22: 'For where two or three are gathered in my name, I am there among them.' For this is a short, pithy saying that is separable from its immediate context.

A number of details suggest that Jesus did envisage some sort of community continuing after his death.

- His sense of sonship and the implicit Christologies of the Synoptics make him the beginning of something new, the dawning of the Kingdom in person, especially shown in his resurrection. He is a new beginning, a new movement. James DG Dunn writes:

  > Jesus is proclaimed as the proclaimer... Jesus so proclaimed God his hearers knew Jesus himself to be the one through whom God comes to expression.
  >
  > *Unity and Diversity in the New Testament*, p. 208

- There is an implicit Christology in his teaching which implies having continuing followers. He is the Shepherd of the sheep, the seeker of the lost coin. He has a people, a flock, to gather in.
- The use of baptism and the Eucharist point to his instituting new rituals of a new community. The early Christians openly boasted two new rituals as innovations, based upon the life and death of Jesus of Nazareth. Baptism was after his baptism, and was an initiation into his death and new life. The logion in Matthew 28:19 about baptising all nations might be post-Easter, but there was some level of continuity between baptism in the life of Jesus and in the early Church. Many things might lie behind the origin of the Eucharist such as the fellowship meals Jesus held with his disciples as expectations of the Messianic banquet to come, and his Last Supper. If the latter was a Passover meal, celebrated independently of the Temple, then Jesus was rejecting the cult of Herod's Temple and was substituting a new rite. Even if this was temporary, even if envisaged to last only a few days until his resurrection and the dawn of the Kingdom, he gave his followers a ritual to last after his death (see Matthew 14:25).

What is clear, though, is that neither Jesus, nor the first Christians envisaged that there would be much of a delay before the end of the age came. They were living in the 'last days', with the world about to be shaken and radically renewed. Any organisational arrangements for their communities were seen as transient and temporary. If someone could travel back and tell Peter and Paul that the Church would last at least 2,000 years, they would have looked at them with stunned disbelief! Early Christianity was thoroughly eschatological. There is no evidence that Jesus left a detailed blueprint for the running of a church. Of course, Christians can argue that the risen Christ guided his disciples in new ways, and the post-Easter logia can be seen as vehicles of inspiration, but they were not part and parcel of the proclamation of the Jesus of history.

2 Jews and Gentiles

> **KEY ISSUE** The first Christians were Jews who did not see any radical difference between themselves and their co-religionists apart from their adherence to Jesus as Messiah.

We have patchy evidence of life in the first, Jerusalem Church, and this comes from sections of the Epistles, Matthew and Acts. Acts is by a Hellenistic Jew or Gentile convert and it tells the story from Paul's theological perspective. It is debatable how historical some of the episodes are, some giving a late date to its composition in the first century, and some earlier. (The book does not say what happened to Paul in the end – it closes when he is awaiting trial in Rome. Some see this as evidence for an early date of authorship.) The document presents a wealth of detail about everyday life and customs in the Hellenistic world, and it is an impressive document for the Classical historians. Some names of minor officials have turned up in inscriptions unearthed by archaeologists, such as the proconsul Gallio in Corinth. Later passages use 'we' as a subject, suggesting that either the author was a travelling companion of Paul, or that he had access to travel diaries. There are also primitive elements in material about the Jerusalem Church in the first nine chapters. The preaching of Peter and the apostles reveals primitive ideas – Jesus is a man empowered by God (Acts 2:22) rather than an incarnate God. The early Christians continue to meet in the Temple courts at the hours of prayer for instruction and fellowship. How far they continued to support the sacrificial cult is debatable, and though they offered sacrifices to make vows and to be ritually pure (note Acts 21:26), there is no definite evidence that they offered expiatory sacrifices any longer. There was a faithful adherence to the Law, as can be seen in Matthew 15:17–19, and the struggles between Gentile converts and Jewish Christians.

These struggles are only touched upon in the New Testament, and perhaps glossed over; we do not have enough evidence to work out what the exact situation was. The incident with Cornelius in Acts 10 shows Peter's surprise, and inner struggle to accept that the Spirit could come upon a non-circumcised Gentile. The visions of the unclean and clean foods, whereby all are declared clean by God (Acts 10:9–16), if historical, would have been radical and upsetting to a devout Jew such as Peter. Acts 6 reveals an earlier struggle within the Jerusalem Church between the Hebrews and the Hellenists – presumably the latter were Hellenistic Jews from the Diaspora who had laxer views than their Palestinian neighbours and whose first language was Greek. The biggest paradigm shift came with the spread of the Gospel among the Gentiles. Jews were used to Gentiles who converted, becoming proselytes, for they followed the Law and were circumcised. Other Gentiles stopped short of this and became God-fearers. It is the latter group who welcomed the Gospel but who saw no point in being circumcised. Could such Gentile Christians thus be incorporated in the people of God, Israel? The Gentile mission was in the hands, largely, of Paul, who made three missionary journeys around the coasts and cities on the Roman trade routes before being arrested in Jerusalem. Paul offers various snippets of autobiographical information, claiming to have been a zealous Pharisee of the tribe of Benjamin, who was from Tarsus, and therefore a Hellenist, but he had also studied the Law in Jerusalem (see Acts 22:3; 2 Corinthians 11:22; Galatians 1:13–14; Philipians 2:5–6). Paul, unusually, was a full Roman citizen. He was born with this honour, and this had been granted to his parents earlier. This gave a person advantages with the law of Rome, and he was allowed to appeal as far as the Emperor, which he did. He was taken to Rome to stand trial. Paul was converted by a vision of the risen Christ, which is recorded in three versions in Acts (Acts 9:1–19; 21:4–16; 26:12–18). He was not one of the original Twelve, nor an eyewitness of the resurrection, and he described himself as one 'untimely born' and as the least of the apostles because of his later experience (1 Corinthians 15:8–9). Was this self-depreciation based upon the mockery of Jerusalem Christians? His stories fill most of Acts, and his seafaring adventures are couched in terms that would remind Greek readers of the epics of Homer. He was truly an apostle to the Gentile world.

a) Acts 15

Acts 15 describes a meeting to settle the matter of Gentile inclusion in the Church/Israel, which reaches a compromise at the Council of Jerusalem. Here, Paul reports to the leaders of the Jerusalem Church, which include James, the brother of Jesus, as well as Peter, James and John. The traditionalists concede that God is blessing the Gentiles, and a bare minimum of Torah observance is laid upon them in Acts 15:20 – to avoid idols and sexual promiscuity, and meat slaughtered in a non-kosher way (this, presumably, included meat sacrificed to pagan gods). They did not have to be circumcised.

It is debatable how historical this is, though, for there is evidence of deeper disagreement between the Jerusalem leaders and Paul in his epistles. Of particular relevance are Galatians 2; 2 Corinthians 11–13 and Acts 21.

b) Galatians 2

Paul confronts Peter when he visits Antioch, a Church with a largely Gentile membership. Eating together, because of the Torah dietary laws, is the issue. Peter seems to relax these at first, but he withdraws when other Jewish Christians arrive from Jerusalem. It is not clear if Paul won the day, for he does not say so, and, in fact, he left Antioch soon after this to begin an independent mission. He was only to return there once more in his lifetime (Acts 18:22). Galatians 2 claims that even Barnabas, his travelling companion, deserted him, and Acts 15:36–40 reveals that they fell out and parted company.

c) 2 Corinthians 11–13

Paul's mission in Corinth is undermined by Jewish Christians from Jerusalem, 'from James'. He insults them as 'false apostles' for they are trying to get Gentile converts to be circumcised. He boasts his own Hebrew ancestry in his defence.

d) Acts 21

This records Paul's final visit to Jerusalem. Interestingly, he is warned by prophets in Tyre not to go, but he does so. In Caesarea he stays with Philip, one of the Hellenists mentioned in Acts 6, and in Jerusalem he stays with Mnason of Cyprus – presumably, also a Hellenist. He does not stay with James! James received him but urges him to prove his loyalty to the Law to disprove rumours about his teaching – which Paul seems happy to do for he has no problem with following the Law voluntarily as a Jew, so long as this is not thought to make a person acceptable to God. When things get out of hand and he is arrested none of the Jerusalem Christians speak out in his defence. James carried influence with the Jews, but he is silent. Acts is also silent about what happened to the collection Paul had organised amongst the Gentile Churches for the Jerusalem Church (1 Corinthians 16:1–4), for famine had reduced many to poverty. It can be assumed that this was not received, as this would have meant recognising the validity of the Gentile mission. The rift between Paul and James might have been that deep.

3 James, brother of the Lord

KEY ISSUE James held considerable power in the Jerusalem Church. He is mentioned several times in the New Testament accounts, as one of the pillars of the Church with Peter, James and John.

1 Corinthians 15:7 has the risen Christ appearing to James (but, significantly, after Peter, and then all the other apostles after James.) Peter is given seniority in some New Testament sources, as 'the Rock' (Matthew 16:18) and the resurrection narratives have Peter as the first disciple to see the risen Lord. Later traditions give James the title 'the Just' (Hebrew: *Zaddik*) and Josephus gives an account of his martyrdom in AD 62. The Church Fathers mention snippets of traditions about James, but they are writing from the second century onwards, and sometimes, as late as the fourth. His death was sometimes seen to be the cause of the fall of Jerusalem in AD 70, and he is described as following a Nazarite vow, neither eating meat, drinking wine, or cutting his hair. Others add that he was celibate, and wore only linen – a reference to a possible High Priestly role.

Robert Eisenman in *James the Brother of Jesus* argues that James was seen as the Opposition High Priest, and his book is full of interesting speculations, though these are highly controversial. He follows the minority view that the Dead Sea Scrolls were written in the first century AD, and that the mysterious Teacher of Righteousness was, in fact, James. The leader of the Qumran community was called the Mebakker, the Overseer, or High Priest of the Community. He also sees the 'Scoffer' in the Scrolls as Paul. He sees James as taking the leadership of the Jerusalem Church rather in the style of a Muslim Caliphate, where the relations of Muhammad succeeded each other. Later sources describe James as the bishop of Jerusalem, and that he was ordained by Jesus himself. Eisenman speculates that the account of the election of a disciple to replace Judas in Acts 1 is a garbled version of James' appointment. More controversially, Eisenman suggests that James was closer to the Jesus of history than Paul in his outlook:

> It is through James, Jesus' spiritual heir and actual physical successor in Palestine, that we are on the safest ground in approaching a historically accurate semblance of what Jesus himself might have been like.
>
> *James the Brother of Jesus*, p.8

His assumption is that Jesus' own flesh and blood would have known his views better than a later convert like Paul. This is to gloss over certain issues, though, for siblings do not always understand each other so well – an outsider or friend might fare better. Paul defends himself by appealing to knowing Jesus in the Spirit, not according to the flesh (2 Corinthians 5:16) – something new has come with the resurrection and the gift of the Spirit. Also, there is an early tradition that the 'brothers' of Jesus were cousins or half-brothers, and this is depicted in some of the apocryphal Gospels. Then again, there seems to have been a rift between Jesus and his family which was only healed after the resurrection (see Mark 3:31–35).

Eisenman points out that James's views were akin to those of the Qumran community, and this would mean that the actions of Jesus when including various outsiders in the Kingdom community would be anathema to him. To follow Eisenman, we would have to discount the multiply-attested tradition of the radical inclusiveness of Jesus in the four Gospels. Surely he goes too far? We simply do not have enough evidence to reconstruct the historical James, or the exact situation in the Jerusalem Church.

A final point of conflict between Paul and James is over '**justification by faith**'. Paul believed that no one could fully obey the Law, and that God's **grace** (unmerited favour) comes to people's aid. They are saved, accepted, by grace, and not by keeping the Law (hence Galatians 3:21–28). By 'justification' Paul means being acceptable to God. The Law is a schoolmaster disciplining and pointing the way until the grace of God came in Christ.

The Epistle of James seems to take issue with this teaching. The idea that any justification can come from faith without good works is rejected (see James 1:22; 2:14–17). Paul, in fairness, was quick to add that *real* faith led to good works, and the evidence of justification was that a person had 'put on Christ' and had changed. Perhaps James was attacking a version of Paul's teaching which was misunderstood and antinomian – lawless. Paul is aware of such criticism and he rejects it in Romans 6:1–4.

4 The heretical Jewish Christians

Later writers describe sects of Jewish Christians surviving, such as the **Nazarenes** and the **Ebionites**. Justin Martyr, writing in the second century, mentions Jewish Christians who followed the Law, but accepted Gentile believers who did not, as well as more zealous **Judaisers** who sought to force the Torah upon all Christians. Once Jerusalem fell, the remaining groups of Jewish Christians seem to have ossified and become harder and stricter. The Nazarenes and Ebionites followed the Torah, praised James and denigrated Paul as an **apostate**, and had more primitive views of Jesus. Their Christology was **adoptionist** – Jesus was a man taken up to God. Epiphanius claims that the Ebionites said that Jesus became 'Christ and Son of God' only at his baptism, and they denied the virgin birth, using only Matthew's Gospel, without the first two chapters. They were also hostile to the Temple cult, perhaps betraying increasing Essene influence after the fall of Jerusalem. James DG Dunn claims that these groups represented a 'stunted, underdeveloped Christianity', and that they are similar and dissimilar to the first Jerusalem Church. The earlier believers were working out their customs and ideas – they were fresh, and developing. The later sects were fixed, frozen and isolated as mainline Christianity developed and adapted to life in the Hellenistic world. There are also clues that these sects had developed ideas that would have been heterodox to the earliest Christians, for the Ebionites appear to have believed that Christ and Jesus were separate beings. The Christ was an archangel who came upon the prophets, and had filled Jesus par excellence. The *Gospel of Thomas* describes James in highly exalted terms as, 'James the Just, for whose sake heaven and earth came into existence ...' Perhaps we should be careful of seeing James and Paul through these later, biased eyes. The NT James was ready to receive Paul and debate with him. Perhaps the gulf was not *so* great at that stage, but the tensions were there. Perhaps early Jewish Christianity had its own factions and currents of thought – how much the 'false apostles' in 2 Corinthians really represented James is open to question. The delay of the ***parousia*** was a crisis, as was the fall of Jerusalem and the need to adapt and react to their surroundings came as a shock, which different people responded to differently. Paul achieved far more than he knew, and his radical and daring vision allowed the Gospel to spread to the Gentile world. AN Wilson in *Paul – The Mind of the Apostle* playfully dubs him the true founder of Christianity, and speculates what would have happened if his Gentile missions had not occurred:

> The whole Jewish inheritance, which is woven inseparably into the Christian religion, would never have been available to the Gentile imagination. The stories which, until our generation, were told to almost every child in the western world, would have been the exclusive preserve of the Jews: Adam and Eve, Noah's Ark, Daniel in the Lion's Den ...

He exaggerates Paul's role in founding Christianity, but he has a point, for the radically inclusive, forgiving God revealed by Jesus finds more of a resonance in Paul than the more uptight, Law-biding Judaisers. Jesus, in the Gospels shows fidelity to the Law but in a radical manner. He feels free, as Messiah, to set aside Old Testament commandments (e.g. Matthew 5:21–22) and to follow the spirit of the Law rather than its letter (e.g. Mk 2:23–28) and he rejected the oral laws that the Pharisees added to the written Law (eg Mk 7:1–8, 14–15). Perhaps Jesus was trying to renew Judaism in a manner that James and other Jerusalem Christians really had not grasped. The new Way was like putting new wine into old wineskins (Mark 2:21–22). Whatever his faults, Paul grasped more of the radical, renewing vision than the other 'pillars of the Church.'

5 Paul the radical

A common Christian stereotype of Judaism is to see it as a legalistic works religion with stern ideas of judgement. This sense stems from some of Paul's writings, where he emphasises grace and the power of Christ to save. What it ignores is the sense of grace that is present in actual, living and ancient Judaism. It also ignores the sense of joy and gratitude that makes a Jew circumcise his child, or participate in a festival. It is not all a legalistic duty and chore. EP Sanders demonstrated this, and Paul's fundamental divergence from mainstream forms of Judaism, in *Paul and Palestinian Judaism* (1977).

He designates both Hellenistic and rabbinic Judaism as a form of 'covenantal nomism', meaning that the Jew was born into, or committed himself or herself to the covenant, and stayed in it by a mixture of good works and repentance. The entire sacrificial cult existed to atone, to forgive transgressions. There was not the Pauline sense of a crushing alienation and inability to achieve acceptance ('righteousness') with God through the Torah. The only source that has similar pessimism is *IV Ezra*, where humans are seen as forever incapable of obeying the Torah. Paul, of course, might have belonged to a now defunct pessimistic school of thought that was advanced by several rabbis; we do not know, but he is out of step with the attitude that most of ancient, and modern Judaism had and has towards the Torah. For Paul, the Torah was a standard, but not a power to change. For the average Jew it was, and is, wisdom, and a gift, which the grace of God helps one to follow. Though no one can ever be perfect before God, his mercy covers the faithful. Paul's form of religion Sanders designated as 'eschatological participation' whereby we are transferred from one aeon into another, from an old creation into a new. The death and Resurrection of Christ, with the gift of the Spirit, achieve this in the believer. The Torah's ethical rules for human relations are still in force, and the fruits of the Spirit in Galatians 5:22–23 follow those precepts. The ritual commandments which deal with human relationship to God are set aside through Christ. Jesus brings a new creation, and the Torah belongs to the old order. For Paul, Jesus is a second Adam, and not a new Moses. His work went deeper, to the most primordial, foundational levels of reality. Sin, for Paul, is not just transgression, but also a power we need deliverance from. Paul's idea of the believer being 'made righteous' by faith is unique – Judaism would only declare someone who was righteous to be so. Even the Qumran community, who came close to Paul's transfer terminology in saying that a convert was one of the righteous, qualified this by expecting faithful obedience to the Torah. Paul's idea of being 'made righteous' is one of his most difficult and controversial doctrines, but, at root, it is the radical idea of acceptance. His sense of pre-Christian angst and failure was healed and forgiven by a touch of divine love. For Paul, the zealous and extreme rabbi, to become acceptable to a loving Father God through Christ was earth-shattering, and it made him create new concepts and placed a new insight into the Christian movement. Sanders agrees:

> It appears that Paul's thought was not simply taken over from any one scheme pre-existing in the ancient world.
>
> *Paul and Palestinian Judaism*, p. 155

There is still a judgement of works in Paul (see 1 Corinthians 3:10–15; 11:29; 2 Corinthians 5:8–10) but works do not save nor bring people into the new covenant. That is by grace. There is the possibility of losing salvation by heinous sin that puts people outside the covenant (see Galatians 5:19 and the warning that people who act in an immoral way will not inherit the Kingdom of God) but some punishment in this life will prevent us from being lost and condemned. Paul is exasperated with some of the early Christians, not just because they have transgressed the standard set in the Torah, but because, if they are in union with Christ, then they should not be in union with the power of sin (see 1 Corinthians 10:1–5 which deals with idols and prostitutes).

Paul blended eschatological participation with covenantal nominism, in fact, and these have blended, with a greater or lesser emphasis on one or the other, at different stages in church history. Churches which follow in an initiation model, of being born into the faith and nurtured as you grow, operate more by a covenantal nominism; those who operate by a conversion model have aspects of the old eschatological awareness of stepping from darkness into light.

James DG Dunn's work *The Theology of Paul the Apostle* hinges on the eschatological shift that Paul sensed as having taken place. Whereas Israel once had a privileged place, and a special gift of the Law, a new covenant was now in force, and grace was freely available to Jews as well as Gentiles. This was an interior work, writing the Law on the heart, to quote the old prophets (e.g. Jer 31:33). The law was not a power of sin, i.e. one of the cosmic powers opposed to God, but an instrument to highlight and determine sin, and as such, it was used by the cosmic powers of sin and death to bring condemnation upon people. Dunn sees Paul as feeling that Israel was 'behind the times', clinging onto ancient privilege with a desire that had become sinful. The law itself was good and holy, though.

Dunn admits that there are aspects of Paul's theology that are not clear, and ambiguities remain. Thus it is not clear whether the 'life-prospering-become-death-dealing function' of the Law, i.e. the transition from the praise of Psalm 119 for the Law to the power of condemnation it wields in Romans, is something intrinsic to the Law's nature, or is to be rooted in Israel's failure to move in step with the eschatological shift. Dunn concludes:

> Or, should we rather say, his theologising always began and ended with the practicalities and little things of human relationships. Paul's theology, however complex and high-flown, was never of the ivory-tower kind. It was first and last an attempt to make sense of the gospel as the key to everyday life and to make possible a daily living which was Christian through and through.
>
> *The Theology of Paul the Apostle*

In other words, Paul thought and wrote 'on the hoof', using letters and not a systematic treatise.

Dunn points out one interesting fragment from Qumran which recasts the language of 'righteousness':

> As for me, if I stumble, the mercies of God shall be my eternal salvation. If I stagger because of the sin of the flesh, my justification shall be by the righteousness of God which endures for ever ... He will draw me near by his grace, and by his mercy will he bring my justification. He will judge me in the righteousness of his truth and in the greatness of his goodness he will pardon all my sins ...
>
> 1QS 11:11–15

This shows that 'the righteousness of God' is akin to 'the faithfulness of God', the covenantal promises to protect, guide and heal. This shows a current in Palestinian Judaism that was not so far away from Paul's language of grace.

6 Pharisees and Sadducees

A final consideration is how the Jesus movement was helped by the rivalries between the Pharisees and the Sadducees. The Christians were another 'philosophy' to use Josephus' terms, and one that had anti-Temple roots, akin to the Essenes and other pious Jews. However, there were points of similarity with the Pharisees:

- The Christians taught the resurrection of the dead, and believed in angels
- They accepted the whole canon of the Old Testament, and not just the Torah as Scripture
- They were happy with the idea that God intervened in human history.

This made the Pharisees more sympathetic at first, and they spoke up for them in the Sanhedrin. Thus, Gamaliel challenged the aristocratic leaders to put the case to a simple test – if the Christians prospered, then God was with them. Otherwise, their movement would peter out, as with that of Judas the Galilean in AD 6.

> Paul was able to use this tension between Pharisees and Sadducees during his arrest in Jerusalem. In Acts 23:6–10, he stirs up the Pharisees in the Sanhedrin to side with his views, claiming 'I am on trial concerning the hope of the resurrection of the dead.'

Summary List

- Jesus spoke of a flock, a people, and gave a ritual meal to remember him by. This suggests that he envisaged some sort of church to continue after him. Early belief in an imminent *parousia* gave way to gradual development of church order as this was delayed. The Jesus of history did not give a detailed blueprint.

- The NT shows that there were early tensions between more closed, ethnic and open ideas of the faith. Paul led the Gentile mission and ran into controversy by insisting that Gentiles need not be circumcised.
- The role of James as leader of the Jerusalem Church is ambiguous. He seems to have been conservative and insular.
- Heretical groups such as the Nazarenes and the Ebionites reveal a stunted Christianity, heavily dependent upon Judaism.
- Paul departed from traditional Jewish understanding of the Law by his sense of eschatological shift from the old aeon to the new. The Law's ritual demands were seen as superseded by Christ, and only its ethical demands were eternal.

Answering structured and Essay questions on Chapter 14

1. List any pieces of evidence from the Gospels that Jesus intended to found a community.
2. Make a chart of the divisions in early Christianity, under the headings: Hellenists; Paul; Jerusalem Church.
3. Read the passages which give autobiographical information regarding Paul. Write a summary of these.
4. Why do some think that James would have understood the teaching of Jesus better than Paul? Is there any evidence for or against this?
5. Can groups such as the Ebionites and the Nazarenes help us to understand what the early Jerusalem Church was like?
6. How did the differences between the Sadducees and the Pharisees help the Church to develop?

14 Epilogue

KEYWORDS

glossolalia – speaking in tongues

incarnation – God took flesh and became man

kerygma – the apostolic preaching/ proclamation

1 Introduction

KEY ISSUE To find the essence of the New Testament, we must seek the original, odd and striking.

There are many different styles of Christian belief and practice displayed in this incomplete and frustrating record of incipient Christianity – clusters of ideas, traditions, Scriptural styles of exegesis and different Christologies. Through this kaleidoscope we can discern consistent outlines, odd, daring and original ideas that shine forth as beacons. This is the genius of Christianity, and if we want to locate divine inspiration in any particular place, let it be here.

One example is the developing belief in the **incarnation**. There might be many parallels with Hellenistic myths and deities, but nothing exact, no perfect match. In fact, the core idea is repugnant to the Greek mind, that God should actually become human, even to the point of suffering. This was a totally new religious idea.

2 Jeremias

It is hard, nonetheless, to say what *the* message of the New Testament is, even by these standards. There are various key themes that are played out, and that interweave. Joachim Jeremias's book, *The Central Message of the New Testament*, presents not one message but several. He selects the following themes:

- God as Abba
- The sacrificial death
- Justification by faith
- The Word

a) God as Abba

God as Abba is about the Father-heart of God, revealed in the inclusion of the outcasts, the people of the land. For the term 'Abba', Jeremias wrote:

> For with Abba we are behind the Kerygma. We are confronted with something new and unheard of which breaks through the limits of Judaism. Here we see who the historical Jesus was: the man who had the power to address God as Abba and who included sinners and the publicans in the kingdom ...
>
> *The Central Message of the New Testament*

He overstated the case, of course, for 'Abba' is attested upon the lips of other Jewish holy men of the time, but the essence of what he says stands true. The radical inclusiveness of the Gospel did overturn tables.

b) The sacrificial death

Jesus' death is special and unique and not just another martyr's death which atones for some sins of the people, but a *universal* atonement for all. The message of Hebrews, for example, was original in its radical stance.

c) Justification by faith

Justification by faith was a novel reworking of Jewish ideas by Paul that elucidated Jesus' words, 'Blessed are the poor, for yours is the kingdom of God'. We are back to the inclusiveness and mercy of God, taking in the unclean and the outcast.

d) The Word

The Word was about revelation, the love and wisdom of God being revealed in Jesus. Jeremias says:

> God has spoken. Jesus of Nazareth is the Word – he is the Word with which God has broken his silence.
>
> *The Central Message of the New Testament*

3 Johnson

Another interesting exploration of early Christianity is by investigating religious experience. Luke Timothy Johnson's *Religious Experience in Earliest Christianity*, Fortress Press (1988) argues that the experiential dimension has been ignored by scholars, who are embarrassed by it, or see it as elusive and speculative. Yet there is enough, robust, official discussion of religious experience in the New Testament that stares us in the face. This is all about the Spirit, and the coming of that Spirit to humanity. It is a power that moves, indwells, is poured out, poured into, that fills, that people drink, that transforms and gives life:

> if the original essence of Christianity was the simple moral teaching of Jesus or the simple theological principle of justification by grace, the register of language I have here catalogued seems as alien as the encroachments of law and organisation from the side of Judaism or the influence of ritual and sacrament from the side of paganism ...
>
> Johnson, *Religious Experience in Earlier Christianity*

Johnson is concerned with the phenomenological approach to religion, where there are different strands and particular types of action and thought across the faiths. The experiential is as vital as that of ritual or doctrine. He sees genuine religious experience as involving four aspects:

- An experience related to the Ultimate
- It involves the whole person – mind, feelings, body and will
- It can have a peculiar intensity
- It will result in action.

A classic example would be the conversion of Paul, though not all such experiences would be so intense. Quieter experience can run deep, but it will result in transformation.

Johnson then studies baptism, **glossolalia** (speaking in tongues) and meals as three shafts to explore the New Testament and its experience of God.

a) Baptism

Power and *communitas* are key elements here. Baptism is a radical inclusion into a new people, no matter what your social origins. It is status-enhancing as a person is empowered and imprinted with new identity. When we recall that the Hellenistic mystery cults were rather elitist, this is striking and daring. The slave and the master were equals as brothers in Christ. Another original twist is the completeness of the initiation. It does not need improving upon, and there is no gradual advancement, no increasing enlightenment as in the mysteries with multiple initiations, or in tribal groups today, or secret societies, such as the Masons with their different degrees and accompanying ceremonies.

b) Glossolalia

This controversial topic takes us straight to the heart of the experiential. There is the aspect of radical inclusion, again, for this gift can be given to rich and poor, Jew and Gentile alike. It is one of the gifts of the Spirit who is poured out upon all who receive Christ. There is also an uneasy sense of it in the New Testament, from the bursting forth of the Day of Pentecost, to the scattered references in Acts, and Paul's concerns tabulated in 1 Corinthians. It is not exactly clear what it is – the ability to speak other languages, or an 'ordered babbling' of a personal prayer language. Paul is worried that it is getting out of hand, and outsiders will feel it is ecstatic frenzy, as in the Pythian spirit of the Delphi oracle. It is interesting that it is the women that most concern him, for women in the Hellenistic world were often thought possessed by the spirit of Apollo, as they sat, receptacle like, over a smoking tripod, and the god entered through the opening of the genitalia and spoke through the other opening of their mouth. Perhaps there are echoes of a threat to deeply ingrained patriarchy here, though there is a wise and general point that 'the spirit of the prophets is subject to the prophets in Christian faith'. Wild, uncontrollable frenzy is pagan and to be spurned. If we learn nothing more at all from this look at glossolalia, we see that Christian religious experience is of a different quality from pagan.

c) Meals

There are different Eucharistic traditions, and types of meal fellowship in the New Testament, but there are common themes of belonging (*communitas*) and boundaries.

- Only those truly initiated can join the feast.
- It is a meal radically open to high and low, so long as they come through Christ, echoing the parables of Jesus about marriage feasts.
- There is a sense of fellowship with Jesus, the one who died and is now risen. He is the living Lord.

Johnson sees the custom of holding eucharists/meals at the tombs of departed brethren as following on from the pagan funerary customs, but resurrection symbolism is to the fore, both in early liturgy and in artefacts and paintings – Jonah and the fish, bread and fish remembering the power of God through Christ in the Gospel stories (feeding the multitude, and huge, surprising catches of fish), descending doves upon chalices and pitchers. The flow of 1 Corinthians 11:23–26 has the command to discern the Body of Christ among the people and the elements, and all drink of the same Spirit.

> so at the very least we might begin to understand how such meals and the elaborate liturgical forms based upon those meals never ceased, from those days to these, to spell magic for those who passed broken

> bread from hand to hand and whispered the name of the One in whose powerful presence they ate.
>
> Johnson, *Religious Experience in Earliest Christianity*

Johnson is critical of scholars who analyse texts and subdivide sources without facing the life-blood, the dynamism of the early Christian movement. He also points out how the history-of-religions school of scholarship is very good at cross-referencing and finding possible parallels from Hellenistic sources, but is obsessed with the etymology of words, and misses the fact that an experience described by two sets of people, using similar terms, might be very different. There is something distinctive about Christian experience of the Spirit that was not there in mystery cults or pagan prophecy – it was incredible power that was controlled and calm, and was open and accessible to all.

4 Conclusion

It would be good to see other studies, drawing out other themes from the NT, such as healing stories. This is another piece of experience. A cursory reading of the healing miracles reveals a familiar theme, that of inclusiveness. It is mainly the socially undesirables (lepers, Romans, women, Gentiles) who are healed.

It would be unfair to speak as though the only bits worth bothering about are the unique ideas. Obviously, the early Church would have had material and beliefs in continuity with Judaism, and would have been influenced by some Hellenistic customs. There is much of moral and spiritual value in the overlap, and we must not follow the example of Perrin's criterion of dissimilarity, whereby only new ideas in the sayings of Jesus are treated as authentic logia. The difference is rich and fascinating, though. Christianity had an originality and a dynamism that made people listen to it as something new. By seeking out its vitality and its new ideas, we can sense something of its real identity. From all that we have said, the radical forgiveness and inclusion of God is central, and this is underscored by the radical involvement of God with his creation in the idea of incarnation. There is a real folly at the heart of the Gospel, a folly that scandalised Jews and Greeks – a Messiah who suffered? – a deity who suffered? And this folly is that of divine love, head over heels in love with the creation.

> For the message of the cross is foolishness to those who are perishing, but to us who are being saved it is the power of God.
>
> 1 Corinthians 1:18

Bibliography

C K Barrett *Jesus and the Gospel Tradition* (SPCK)
M Borg *The Lost Gospel Q* (Ulysses Press)
G Bornkamm *Jesus of Nazareth* (Hodder & Stoughton)
F F Bruce *New Testament History* (Anchor)
Brueggeman, W *The Bible and Post Modern Imagination*
R Bultmann *A Theology of the New Testament*, Vol. 1 (SCM)
B S Childs *Introduction to the Old Testament as Scripture* (SCM)
B Chilton and J Neusner *Judaism in the New Testament* (Routledge)
D Cohn-Sherbot *The Jewish Heritage* (Basil Blackwell)
J D Crossan *The Historical Jesus – The life of a Mediterranean Jewish Peasant* (Harper Collins)
O Cullmann *The Christology of the New Testament* (SCM)
J D G Dunn *Unity and Diversity in the New Testament* (SCM)
R Eisenman *James the Brother of Jesus*
J K Elliot *The Apocryphal New Testament* (Oxford, Clarendon)
F V Filson *A New Testament History* (SCM)
Funk, Hoover and the Jesus Seminar *The Five Gospels* (Macmillan)
B Gerhardsson *The Origins of the Gospel Traditions* (SCM)
M D Goulder *Midrash and Lection in Matthew* (SPCK)
J Hayes *An Introduction to Old Testament Study* (SCM)
M Hengel *The Atonement*
M Hengel *The Son of God* (SCM)
J Hick (ed.) *The Myth of God Incarnate* (SCM)
M Hilton and G Marshall *The Gospels and Rabbinic Judaism* (SCM)
J Jeremias *The Central Message of the New Testament*
J Jeremias *Theology of the New Testament* (SCM)
T Johnson *Religious Experience in Early Christianity* (Fortress Press)
Jung *Memories, Dreams and Reflection* (Fontana)
Kirk *Myth: It's Meaning and Functions in Ancient and Other Cultures* (Cambridge)
W Klassen *Judas – Betrayer or Friend of Jesus?*
B Lindars *The Son of Man* (SPCK)
T Ling *A History of Religion East and West* (Macmillan)
E Lohmeyer *Galiläa un Jerusalem* (Göttingen)
B J Mahina and R Rohrbaugh *Social Science Commentary on the Synoptic Gospels* (Fortress)
T W Manson *The Servant Messiah* (Cambridge)
I H Marshall (ed.) *New Testament Interpretation* (Paternoster)
J Miller *Jesus at Thirty* (Fortress)
J Moltman *The Crucified God* (SCM)
C F D Moule *The Origin of Christology* (Cambridge)
W Pannenberg *Jesus, God and Man* (SCM)
P Perkins *Reading the New Testament* (Paulist)
N Perrin *Rediscovering the Teaching of Jesus* (SCM)
J Rees Larcombe *An Unexpected Healing* (Hodder)

J A T Robinson *Can we Trust the New Testament?* (Mowbray)
J A T Robinson *Redating the New Testament* (SCM)
J M Robinson *A New Quest of the Historical Jesus* (SCM)
E P Sanders *The Historical Figure of Jesus* (Penguin)
Paul and Palestinian Judaism (SCM)
A Schweitzer *The Quest of the Historical Jesus* (SCM)
E chweitzer *Jesus the Parable of God* (SCM)
G Stanton *Gospel Truth* (Fount)
C Talbert *What is a Gospel?* (SPCK)
G Theissen *The Shadow of the Galilean* (SCM)
G Theissen and A Merz *The Historical Jesus – A Comprehensive Guide* (SCM)
H E Tödt *The Son of Man in the Synoptic Tradition* (SCM)
G Vermes *Jesus the Jew* (Fount)
G Vermes *Jesus and the World of Palestinian Judaism* (SCM)
G Vermes *The Dead Sea Scrolls in English* (Penguin)
A N Wilson *Paul – The Mind of the Apostle*

Further Reading

What is the New Testament

J K Elliott, *The Apocryphal New Testament* (Oxford, Clarendon) is the most recent and thorough collection of non-canonical gospels. This is based on the earlier edition by M R James. Dip into *The Five Gospels* (Macmillan) by Funk, Hoover and the Jesus Seminar to see what they make of the *Gospel of Thomas.*

The Hellenistic world

See Pheme Perkins, *Reading the New Testament* (Paulist), for more on the Hellenistic background. Consult Apuleius, *The Golden Ass* (OUP) for details of a mystery cult.
The essay, 'Two Roots or a Tangled Mass?' by Frances Young in *The Myth of God Incarnate* (ed. John Hick, SCM) discusses the similarities in the beliefs about rulers and divine men and Christian belief. She also points out what is odd and distinctive in Christian confessions about Jesus – that God became incarnate. Hellenism suggested that a god might disguise himself, temporarily, as a human, or that a person could be half god/half human, but never that God *really* became human.

Judaism at the time of Jesus

Good background information can be gleaned from F F Bruce *A New Testament History* (Anchor), or Floyd Filson *A New Testament History* (SCM). Josephus refers to the parties in first century Judaism in both *The Jewish War* (Penguin Classics) and *the Antiquities of the Jews.* The relevant references are as follows:
– The Pharisees: *JW* ii, 162ff; *Ant* xiii, 172, xviii, 13.
– The Sadducees: *JW* ii, 163ff; *ant* xiii, 173, xviii, 16f.
– The Essenes: *JW* ii, 119f; *ant* xviii, 18ff.
– The Zealots: *JW* ii, 441, 651, iv 160f; *Ant* xviii, 8.

Use of the Old Testament

The Gospels and Rabbinic Judaism (SCM) by Rabbi Michael Hilton and Fr. Gordan Marshall has a wealth of rabbinic parallels with the teaching of Jesus. M Goulder *Midrash and Lection in Matthew* (SPCK) suggests that Matthew was an expansion of Mark by *midrash.*
E P Sanders *Paul and Palestinian Judaism* (SCM) outlines the culture of the day and the influences upon Paul and the early Church.

What is apocalyptic?

Pheme Perkins provides a concise account of apocalyptic in *Reading the New Testament* Paulist). Trevor Ling, *A History of Religion East and West* (Macmillan), is highly accessible but rather dated. There is useful material, too, in Hayes, *An Introduction to Old Testament Study* (SCM).

The search for the historical Jesus

The Historical Jesus – A Comprehensive Guide (SCM) by Gerd Theissen and Annette Merz is an up-to-date and thorough introduction to all the issues and arguments. This sets out material in easily readable and digestible sections, summarising different positions. It can be dipped into as a reference book at several stages in a course on the NT. The Q material has been collected together into a narrative in *The Lost Gospel Q* edited by Marcus Born (Ulysses Press). See what impression of Jesus this text gives you on its own. (There is a very good critical introduction to studies about Q, also). Pheme Perkins and Floyd Filson give good overviews of Source, Form and Redaction Criticism (see Bibliography). Walter Brueggemann, *the bible and Post Modern Imagination,* explores the texts as literary pieces which affects the reader in certain ways. B S Childs, *Introduction to the Old Testament as Scripture* (SCM), gives more details about canonical criticism, and links with the NT. Bruce J and Malina and Richard L Rohrbaugh, *Social Science Commentary on the Synoptic Gospels* (Fortress), provides a wealth of sociological analysis. John Miller, *Jesus at Thirty* (Fortress), presents a credible psychohistorical study of the Gospels. Geza Vermes, *Jesus the Jew* (Fount), could also be consulted. Bruce Chilton and Jacob Neusner, *Judaism in the New Testament* (Routledge), is worth dipping into, though it is rather advanced. Try the first chapter to get a general overview.

The death of Jesus

Consult Gerd Theissen and Annette Merz, *The Historical Jesus – A Comprehensive Guide* (SCM), ch. 14.

Miracle stories

Jennifer Rees Larcombe is an example of a modern Christian who believes that the power of prayer healed her of encephalitis, an inflammation of the brain that left her in a wheelchair for years. Her story is told in *An Unexpected Healing* (Hodder).

The virgin birth and the Resurrection

Read the final section of E P Sanders, *The Historical Figure of Jesus* (Penguin).

Did Jesus intend to found the Church?

James D G Dunn, *Unity and Diversity in the New Testament* (SCM), pp. 235–66, gives a useful overview of tensions in the early Church. Dunn's *The Theology of Paul the Apostle*, is a huge tome that is well worth dipping into. His conclusions about the Law are to be found on pp. 59–161. Robert Eisenman, *James the Brother of Jesus* is overly long and repetitious, but pp. xvii–xxxvi and 185–213 give a good sense of his arguments. Joachim, Jeremias, *The Central Message of the New Testament*, pp. 51–70, covers justification by faith. Consult E P Sanders, *Paul and Palestinian Judaism* (SCM), pp. 543–56, for the contrast between Paul and the Judaism of his day. A N Wilson, *Paul – The Mind of the Apostle*, is controversial, but well-written and full of background material. His first chapter sets the scene. This work is spoilt by the author's overly sceptical attitude to faith as he was writing as a lapsed Christian; there are many illuminating details, though.

Index